JAMES HENRY MOSER
HIS BRUSH AND HIS PEN
by
GRACE MOSER FETHEROLF

James Henry Moser

Uncle Remus

FETHEROLF PUBLISHING

ACKNOWLEDGMENTS AND CREDITS

Special appreciation is extended to the following. GRACE MOSER FETHEROLF for the compilation and title of her father's biography. ROSEMARY BREEN WITHERS — material from her book, ''The Landscapes of J. H. Moser.'' JAMES FETHEROLF — research and additional material from the Moser files. SAMUEL FETHEROLF — research, editing and picture selection. ROSE HUSON — typing and assistance in editing. ELIZABETH LLOYD — photography and typing.

Special Credits: D. APPELTON AND COMPANY, New York, N.Y. Moser sketches from ''Uncle Remus'' by Joel Chandler Harris published in 1881 — 22-23-29-Title Page. PRANG PUBLISHERS, Boston, Mass. Prints of Moser Originals ''Supper Time'' — 33B, ''The Book Worm'' — 29, and Washington Calendar 1890 — 40-41-48-52-94. HARPER AND BROTHERS PUBLISHERS, New York, N.Y. Moser Illustrations ''The Whistler,'' ''The Moonshiner'' and ''Cotton Is King'' — 36A-37. *THE WASHINGTON PRESS* — 48. *THE WASHINGTON TIMES, THE POST* and *THE HERALD*, Moser Art Essays as noted.

Picture Credits — Public Collections: NATIONAL MUSEUM OF AMERICAN ART, SMITHSONIAN INSTITUTION, Washington, D.C. — 121. NATIONAL PARK SERVICE, JEFFERSON NATIONAL EXPANSION MEMORIAL NATIONAL HISTORIC SITE, St. Louis, Missouri — 50-51. CORNWALL HISTORICAL SOCIETY, Cornwall, Connecticut — 7-8A-11-31-33A-38-54-55-57-58-99-125-Back Cover. SAN JACINTO MUSEUM OF HISTORY ASSOCIAITON, La Port, Texas — 11-13-14. THE WILLARD MEMORIAL LIBRARY, Evansville, Indiana — 124. (Photo by William Sonntag.)

Picture Credits — Private Collections: JAMES FETHEROLF — 6 - 8B - 21-24-25-26-27-29-30-36B-37-39-41-45-53-58A-59B-63-67-74-80-81-83-84-85-93-115-119A-120-129-136. SAMUEL FETHEROLF — Front Cover-9-15-20-28-33B-35-47-69-71-75-77-79-86-89-91-101-105-111-119B-131-141. RALPH FETHEROLF — 3-19-23-25-56-73-109-137. ROBERT GRIGGS — 64-65-87-97-113-127-133-135. DAVID GRIGGS — 59A-76-103-107. MARTHA GRIGGS AICHELE — 5. EDWARD FETHEROLF — 49-85-117-123-139. MARTHA FETHEROLF LOUTFI — 43-95-106. JOHN RICKEY — 17. PAULA HOLMES — 36A.

CONTENTS

JAMES HENRY MOSER
HIS BRUSH AND HIS PEN

by

GRACE MOSER FETHEROLF

THE CENTURY MAGAZINE
January 27, 1903

Dear Mr. Moser:

As a slinger of ink, you take no odds from your brush. I'm surprised to see you are so much of a "literary fellow" but then, why not? A man who can tell a story as well as you do with the latter tool, should be able to do as well with the former. . . .

Signed — W. Lewis Fraser

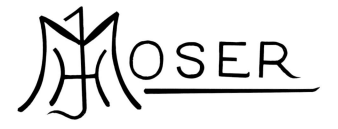

FOREWORD

In compiling this biography of James Henry Moser, my father, I, for the most part, let him speak for himself from the wealth of letters, art notes, and other material which he carefully filed, or to which I have fallen heir from friends.

My personal recollection is of a man demonstratively affectionate, with arms flung wide to greet the family upon his return from the studio; always quick to "turn a phrase" for smiles or laughter, and constantly bubbling with anecdotes and dialect stories. He was an inimitable mimic.

Always boyish, he seemed like a brother to us. I remember how pleased he was when I once remarked that our minister, Dr. Newman (a dear friend of the family), seemed more like my father and he more like my big brother. When my sister once called him "Daddy Boy" he was so pleased that ever afterward he cherished the name and always signed his letters to us "D.B."

His paintings, through the years, have become few where the public can enjoy them although the National Collection of Fine Arts in Washington has four and the Corcoran Gallery two. While they were frequently "on the line" in exhibitions with other great names of the time, they were usually not large "gallery" pictures but pictures for the home — to be lived with and loved as windows opening on the beauties and mysteries of nature. One might look at them, but more important, he felt them.

In spite of the fact that James Henry Moser had little formal education, he came to be considered a well educated man. From his early youth he sought friendship with cultured people, and whenever anyone alluded to or quoted from a classic, he immediately looked up that classic and read it. What is more, he remembered what he read and could quote from it.

Democratic and friendly, his friends covered a wide range, from keepers of the Baltimore and Ohio canal locks with whom, on his sketching trips, he had long confidential chats; to his patrons who numbered among them several United States Presidents, and the great Alexander Graham Bell.

Grace Moser Fetherolf.
— 1967 —

TO JAMES HENRY MOSER

What Grecian goddess did to you
    This wondrous gift impart,
So natural that we hesitate
    To call it only art?

You paint an evening so that we
    May feel its subtle hush;
A wave, as though that wave itself
    Had broken from your brush.

If you, yourself, are strong as are
    The waves you love so much;
And if your heart be true and light
    As is your fingers' touch.

To know you well would make more smooth
    Rough ways we all have trod;
A man so near to nature must
    Live very close to God.

James G. Burnett

From Editorial page, *Washington Post*
Sunday — February 20, 1891

3

Joel Chandler Harris

JAMES HENRY MOSER — JULY 1890

A PAINTER'S DREAMS

"There is nothing more delightful in the whole range of a painter's experience than his dreams — those visions of harmony which swarm in his busy brain. Nothing is so humble or even ugly in nature that it does not hold some hint of beauty which breeds in his fancy a picture. These pictures follow one another so fast they are like the dissolving views of the stereopticon, for one conception melts into another with such rapidity that in almost any ramble, if his mind be in tune, the painter meets with pictures enough to keep his brush busy for a year."

Washington Times. January 7, 1900.
James Henry Moser.

PICTORIAL ART

"As life is a little concrete segment of the great mystery beyond which the imagination plays with hope or fear, so pictorial art is a limitless, uncertain thing, as craft is not; however, much the unknowing would have us think them identical.

"When a skilled craftsman with power to perceive the greater truths hidden in the universe, creates upon canvas something that awakens in the beholder the same emotions he himself has experienced, the painter is an artist. It is not important that one concerns himself with form, another with color, another with contrasts of light and shade, and still others with the story or moral, but adds to the variety of expression and point of view. The art question involved must always rest upon the value of the interpreter's revelation. This may be very great in a picture where people see only astonishing craft and a pleasing story."

Washington Post. March 11, 1906.
James Henry Moser.

AMERICAN WATER COLOR SOCIETY

"Congratulations — Elected member of the Society."
Signed — F. Hopkinson Smith.
March 15, 1899.

The above telegram was received in his Washington studio by James Henry Moser, an artist who had thus won the distinction of becoming the first member of the "American Water Color Society" residing outside of New York City; a man who worked tirelessly for good art in the Nation's Capitol through his pictures, his pen, and through a notable class in water color at the Corcoran Gallery of Art.

Curiously enough, he won this honor not by a large important painting, but by a group of eleven small water colors measuring only five by eight inches each called the January Thaw Series. A strong draftsman, emotionally mature in his feeling for nature, he brought to the small pictures the same strength and breadth of treatment contained in his larger works. From his early years he had delighted in making small pictures, even miniatures one to three inches long — it could almost have been called a hobby — and many were his friends who, in his later years, treasured small "gems" received in letters.

Moser was a versatile painter, using from time to time widely differing methods, but though he occasionally painted in oil and pastel, his real love was water color. In this medium he portrayed delicate spring tones with infinite sweetness or gloried in the brilliant richness of fall, but his real delight was in the cool tones of mountains shrouded in cloud, or rising stark from mist-filled valleys; or in days of mist and rain, "gray days," he called them, which he studied direct from nature completely clad in a waterproof outfit.

J. H. Moser

LINGERING DRIFTS — *ONE OF THE JANUARY THAW PAINTINGS*

In Moser's own story he said, ''In 1897 the American Water Color Society rejected all four of the pictures I sent them. I did not murmur, but determined to be on hand the next year with something the jury would want, and want very much. A year later I was able to send eleven pictures — hoping that some two or four at most — they are small — might be accepted. The jury hung them all in a group in the main gallery at the National Academy of Design.''

These pictures, some of Moser's most exquisite snow scenes, apparently prompted his election to membership in the American Water Color Society the following year.

The *New York Times* 1899 in a review of the exhibition said that Moser's Water Colors were among the most notable things shown and adds that four were sold in New York.

JAMES CHOOSES AN ART CAREER

JAMES HENRY MOSER was born in Whitby, Ontario, Canada, January 1, 1854, the older son of John and Matilda Gordon Moser. John Moser was an architect and later became widely esteemed in the early years of the "American Institute."

His work eventually took him to Columbus, Ohio, where he moved with his family in 1864. He would have liked to have his sons take up the study of architecture, but James would have none of it, and long before he finished his meager schooling spent all his spare time sketching, painting and haunting the studios of the town's artists: Witt, Cookman, Frederick Church, Frank Miller and Prof. Schroeder, with whom he made friends and doubtless gained much valuable information although it is questionable whether he actually studied with any of them.

It was in Toledo, where John Moser moved with his family in 1875 that James began his professional career with a studio of his own in the Ketchum bank building. James later wrote of this period: "Frank Scott was the art leader of the town and a most devoted and helpful friend to me. Kenyon Kox was nineteen, Harvey Lungren also under twenty while I was twenty-two. Our parents resided in Toledo and we were close, sympathetic chums, dreaming of art in its most modern aspects in an atmosphere conventional, deaf and blind to the newer movement that was developing and broke with the Centennial Exposition in Philadelphia." James went to the Exposition in June, and his sketchbook of that period contains sketches of points of interest in Philadelphia as well as at the Exposition; and continues with sketches made in New York, during a trip up the Hudson by day boat, and in Albany.

6

1876 CENTENNIAL SKETCH BOOK　　*J. H. Moser*

"Federal Hill" May '92
J. H. Moser
Baltimore

FORT McHENRY — BALTIMORE

J. H. Moser

MEETING MARTHA

In April of the following year, 1877, James opened his studio door one morning to three callers: Mrs. Allen, a friend of his, and two strangers — Mrs. Hubbard, a plump dark woman in middle youth, and Miss Scoville, a young lady so startlingly lovely that, for a moment, he was at a loss for words. She was willowy and beautifully dressed, with soft golden-brown hair, green-gray eyes and a winning though somewhat timid smile. ''The prettiest thing I ever saw,'' he always said afterwards.

Mrs. Hubbard, herself an artist and the mother of two small children, had come with her cousin from Connecticut to make arrangements for painting lessons during her stay. James was delighted at the prospect of having the beautiful Martha Scoville as a pupil, and arrangements were promptly made which eventually developed a friendship not only with his pupil, but with Mrs. Hubbard as well. It was not long before he found himself dropping into the Hubbard home frequently, where he came to enjoy the family, and where he got much motherly and professional advice from Mrs. Hubbard. As for Martha, she was a talented pupil, and as the weather became milder, the lessons frequently became outdoor sketching trips enjoyable to both.

She was always secretly amused at his attempts at the ''Bohemian'' in dress: the white silk hat so large it almost rested on his ears, his flaring windsor tie, and clothes usually a size too large and verging on the extreme. He, however, never questioned his feeling for Martha, and during a sketching trip at the end of her stay, on June 23rd, though he was still living with his parents and had little to offer, he burst bounds and proposed marriage to her. Her answer, while not encouraging, did not shut out all hope; but it took seven long years and endless beautiful miniature paintings and sketches sent to her in letters, before she was fairly won.

8

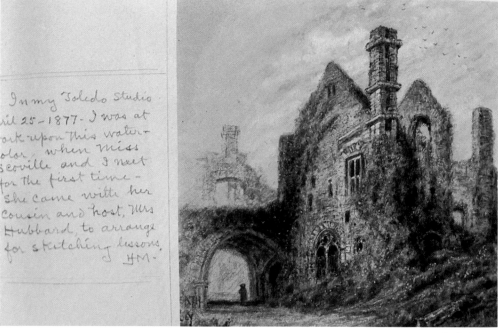

In my Toledo studio April 25 - 1877 - I was at work upon this water-color, when Miss Scoville and I met for the first time - She came with her cousin and host, Mrs Hubbard, to arrange for sketching lessons. J.H.M -

J. H. Moser

J. H. Moser

9

ENTRANCE TO SCOVILLE FARM

J. H. Moser

MOVE TO GALVESTON
AND THE TORNADO

In that same spring, 1877, John Moser moved with his wife and two younger children, Eda and George, to Galveston, Texas, where he was to superintend the building of the Cotton Exchange of which he was the architect. Augusta, the older daughter, had married Alfred Zucker, a promising young architect, while the family was still living in Columbus, and they had gone to New Orleans to live. James followed the Moser family later, set up a studio, and was at once in love with the tropical luxuriance of the foliage, the quaint semi-Spanish character of some of the houses and the wonderful beach of unbroken sand.

Many years later, in an article for the *Washington Times*, James recalled his early impressions of Galveston. "I saw heavily laden orange trees higher than two story buildings, and pink blossomed oleander trees forming complete arches over the pavements of some blocks. Cisterns were everywhere. There was no other water supply at that time. These cisterns rested on open framework high in the air, where they supplied water to the more important houses, but in humbler yards cisterns were little above the level of the ground. The residences, with very few exceptions, were built of wood, as was also the curbing on most of the streets. I was captivated by the paintableness of everything. It was a new kind of picturesqueness, and the treeless stretch of sand melting into the horizon to the southward had a peculiar fascination to me. It suggested Robinson Crusoe and swarthy pirates.

"Some live-oaks and magnolias thrived, but salt cedars — a willowy sort of cedar that bore a pink blossom, seemed the most at home there, and added greatly to the charm of the place. Cacti of low growth and palmetto grew sparsely in ragged spots on the edge of town. Bananas and the high palmettos loomed up where they were cultivated about the houses. These homes where vegetation was encouraged were surrounded with a rank growth of plants of every description."

He goes on to describe a tornado that came the second year they were living in Galveston.

"One can easily imagine what havoc a tornado would make of all that luxuriant growth. It was one of the most melancholy sights I remember having seen. But the sea! It was sublime and most weirdly fascinating!

"I had been warned to keep away from the seashore, for my fondness for it in stormy weather was known at home, but it was useless. Unmindful of the rain, I went seaward along the east end, wading where I had to — the streets were all rivers — until I reached a point where there was an open board fence leading out onto the shore. As the water grew deeper and the wind more fierce, I climbed to the top of the fence and crawled out cautiously toward the foothills of the sea as far as I dared. The foam and swash broke about my knees as I clung to a post, straining my eyes to study the mighty fringe of that angry sea. Scanning the rainy depths of the inky blue sky, out of which came madly tearing in one green wave after another, like mimic sharp peaked mountains of liquid plate glass with the quality of color one observes looking down the green depths of the edge of thick window plate, I was overcome by its tragic and bewildering beauty. All thought of fear left me. My enjoyment was intense. The color was in every shade of marine green, falling away into steely tones, where the rain and sky enveloped the great waves like a dissolving view on a screen. Now and then a wave higher than the rest would loom up out of the mist, and with uncanny white edge of foam seem sure to sweep over me. But, bumping and jostling against counter waves, its great

11

J. H. Moser

AN ADOBE HOUSE — SAN ANTONIO, TEXAS — 1878

bulk would wear away until it was lost and mingled with the savage current which flowed like a torrent past my fence.

"Nothing moves in such graceful lines as water. The greater the bulk, the more splendid and inspiring is the grace of line and angle. After two hours of rapturous watching, the boards of my fence reaching out into the sea began to loosen and bang against my post and I was brought to my senses and returned reluctantly home.

"The next day I began a big picture in oil of that sea, and worked upon it for months afterwards, but an over-anxiety to get the detail prevented me from telling the story of that furious and mighty ocean of water as it stormed toward me.

"The painter does not learn easily to recognize and grasp the big things in his subject, though he may feel them. Perhaps I should have known, but I did not, that to attempt to paint the detail of that sea would rob it of thrilling grandeur and movement. As a consequence of my ignorance, that patient and honest effort, one of the largest and most elaborate oil paintings I ever made, was a dismal failure."

TRIP NORTH TO NEW YORK AND BOSTON
December 1, 1878

I have just returned from a seven-week trip north (by sea both ways). I am weary from the tiresome voyage. My trip north was a pleasant one, part of the expense was borne by business in connection with some engraving — railroad cuts.

I took with me about thirty water colors. The dealer in New York on Nassau Street proved a useful friend for he is an old dealer who knows all the "ins" and "outs" of the business. He had pictures by William Hart, Cropsey and Topham, but though his paintings contained only gems by known and coming artists, the mass of them are pretty pictures that one can neither praise nor condemn. He pronounced my water colors extra, but said there were so many of them he would advise me to try the big uptown dealers adding, "If they buy them they will pay you more than anyone else, but you will find it hard to suit them and I wouldn't advise you to go if I didn't think these things full of merit." I selected ten of the best large and small, and marched up to Goupel and Co's, called for the buyer, Mr. Ross, explained my mission, was invited courteously to bring the pictures (all nicely mounted on heavy cardboard) into the back office, then we talked. He finally said he would like to consult Mr. Knoedler and asked me to call later. The water color room is underneath the main gallery and there is a descent of three or four steps as you enter it. The walls were covered with choice figure pictures and some fine landscapes. I sold him all I showed him, ten. Two marines and one of hanging moss he liked best, so framed and hung them. He seemed anxious to handle all the pictures I send to New York, so that is the bargain for the present.

I went to Williams and Everett in Boston, and did better with them — sold them the balance of the collection. Mr. Williams treated me well, seemed surprised to meet with art from that section of the country, and promised big things for me as a watercolorist. Mr. Atwood, Vice-President of the Art Club of Boston, who had seen the picture, was introduced to me by Mr. Williams and talked to me very earnesty, pressing my hand as though he meant it. Says he, "Stick to water-color, I like your method and I love watercolor and am sorry they are not more appreciated."

13

J. H. Moser

THE ALAMO — 1878

The Mosers remained in Galveston for two years, and it was during this time that the terrible yellow fever epidemic broke out in New Orleans. Sister Gussie's husband, Alfred Zucker, was stricken early and Gussie nursed him back to health then took it herself and died. It was a severe blow to all the family. Alfred left New Orleans shortly after this and made his home in Vicksburg, Mississippi, where the Mosers also moved in the spring of 1879.

J. H. Moser

THE MOSERS MOVE TO VICKSBURG, MISSISSIPPI
April 10, 1879.

We made the trip from Galveston by boat. After crossing the Gulf we landed at Morgan City, a picturesque combination of fruit stands, country notion stores, cabins, and a white-washed church, all on the bayou. The railroad trip from there to New Orleans was through the great sugar country, cyprus trees draped with moss, palmettos among the undergrowth, and cane. I will try to write you a fair description of the Mississippi steamboat trip on the "Robert E. Lee." We had barely time to scramble aboard, our stay in New Orleans being rather a matter of minutes than hours.

Coming up the river, the scenes from "Uncle Tom" had a kind of realization, the landscape part, in the sugar-house chimneys and presses showing above the cane and cypress. Ma, Eda and I had the nicest, quietest bit of travelling those two days that we had ever experienced. The passenger list was small, some few northerners, who were very pleasant, and the southerners were kind too. In fact, eating at table together and promenading, we became very friendly.

Jeff Davis was among the passengers. The first afternoon I was sitting at the bow with my feet on the rail, sketching now and then bits of cottonwood and canebrake, when John Cannon whose father is the famous steamboat man, owner of the "Lee," came over and said, "Moser, want to see Jeff Davis?" "Jeff Davis? Yes. Sure, where is he?" "There," said he pointing to an old man with a thin face, bright blue eyes and a remarkably cheerful expression. I had a memorable talk with him. He is a charming old gentleman, a modest unassuming talker, extremely entertaining, dressed in black with crepe, mourning for his son lost last summer. Fever. I introduced Eda and showed him a picture of Gussie I carry in my watch. Tears filled the old gentleman's eyes as he studied the picture, said consoling things to sister and wrote in her autograph album. He left us at one of his plantations near here.

15

STREAM IN THE MEADOW (Oil — 9 × 11¾)

J. H. Moser

VICKSBURG, MISSISSIPPI — 1879

We had some gorgeous sunsets, and the young cottonwoods with their sprinkling of green made wonderful spring pictures — wish you could see my sketch book. Full! Memoranda enough for a year. The question is becoming not one of material, but time to work it up. At present the bread-and-butter question takes the lead. I declare for it, just as a fellow thinks that question is under his thumb and he can strike out and experiment with his prospects — make art, in my case, he finds he has to knuckle down to that thing which will make the most money now, and make it surely.

We have been in Vicksburg some time now and are delighted with the place and the people. I was glad enough to leave Galveston. Indeed, anything that looks like a step nearer the north is welcome to me. Two whole years among the shipping, tropical vegetation, and by the beach, was ample time for me to sketch and study. You cannot imagine how homesick I became for hills and tall trees. Evening after evening I have taken rides on Alfred's pony, Prince, till there remains hardly a road in any direction that I have not explored. You have no idea how charming the roads are. Mississippi to me has always seemed a dismal place, a land of darkies, cotton and corn. Instead, with all these unmistakable marks of its "southhood" there are many places which remind me of the hills along the Ohio, or spots in Pennsylvania, if it were not for the trees in mourning. The hanging moss is lovely in some instances, then again it has a harsh, desolate look, dignified and lonesome.

I joined the Methodist Church here which I have been promising Ma to do, but don't see but what, save for a shade of earnestness, I shall be the same "Jolly Jeems." I have always been a Methodist from the time I sat on the benches with my boots, copper-toed, ten inches from the floor. The Sunday School here is in a more flourishing condition than one might imagine from reading accounts of pistol-play here in Mississippi. They also have a Y.M.C.A. here that has especially entertaining meetings that have helped me very much in forming congenial acquaintances.

Pa is out at Meridian looking after a court house, and Alfred went out to Jackson this afternoon at three, to see Gov. Stone of this state concerning the Mississippi Agricultural College building. There are a very nice, high-toned set of people here. I have a circular out that will help me to become better acquainted; and I hope too, in this way, to become introduced to people who will buy my watercolors, for I do not want to waste any time on oil portraits, they take up so much valuable daylight.

I am very busy sketching darkies, so many are leaving for Kansas, and as they leave I have a fine opportunity. They have been treated dreadfully, swindled in many instances by the merchants and planters until this result is most natural. However, they are such an ignorant lot, they cannot expect to be better off unless they get honest men to direct them wisely. They are strong, tremendously muscular men whose labor must be enormously productive if properly managed, and their wants very simple, representing almost no money.

SETTING THE BOX TRAP

J. H. Moser

BRINGING HOME THE POSSUMS

J. H. Moser

To Mrs. Hubbard. Vicksburg, Mississippi.
June 1, 1879

It does seem as though my plans were hopeless and as though fate had nothing better to do than to amuse herself trying to see how far she could go spoiling my schemes. Here I have worked last winter and this spring hoping to have saved enough money to give me this entire summer in Cornwall sketching and working up pictures from nature; and then money enough still to make a substantial start in New York where I could give the studio-in-a-great-city question a fair trial. Well, that money was earned and loaned to my brother Alf to pay off debts incurred during the yellow fever epidemic as well as since. Business prospects have not proven all he had anticipated, and Pa is disappointed in Vicksburg. He is delighted with those of Mattie's letters that he has seen, and has as high hopes of a bright future for me as I have myself, and consequently is grieved at anything standing between that bright day and me.

I have gone pretty actively into portrait work; it's no use talking, there's the most money in that. No man can study what he likes or what pleases him until he has money and is thereby independent. I am concentrating my forces and I think the result will be satisfactory even though I have to sacrifice some good things by the way.

THE MOSERS MOVE TO ATLANTA

In June of 1879 John Moser obtained building contracts for a Cotton Exchange and Cathedral (St. Mark's) in Atlanta, Georgia. James went with him, and in order to bring his own name before the public, placed a large number of his paintings on exhibition. The following is from the *Atlanta Constitution*.

The new arrival, Mr. Moser, has many of his pictures on exhibition at Goodman's on Whitehall Street. There an idea may be gained of this young artist's versatility and fine spirited style of work. Speaking faces and lovely landscapes in oil whose beauty grows as you examine them, flower pieces delicately painted in water color, also bits of sea and land done in the same, with others in black-and-white; and portfolios full of sketches; all showing the same free, bold hand and the same spirited mode of treatment. There are some sketches of the negro "exodus" which he has ready to send to Harper's (for whom much of his work is done) which are full of humorous suggestion and extremely well conceived. Mr. Moser is a Canadian we believe, though he has been at work for some time in the southwest, and is just from Vicksburg. He looks like a Louisiana Creole with his olive skin, speaking jet black eyes, and expressive gesticulation.

To Mrs. Hubbard.
September 23, 1879.

I am more occupied hand and brain, than ever before in my whole life. The necessity for activity never seemed so plain to me. I find so much more ready to my hand that I can accomplish that I lose no time in speculation. No place seems dreary to me, strange or incomplete, for "My love maketh loveliness" of all I see and do.

19

CUPID BEGGING

J. H. Moser

I set out when I left Toledo, in pursuit of Mattie's happiness and my own. If I find in the end that I have been hunting something as visionary as the famed ''Pot of Gold'' at the foot of the rainbow, I shall be blessed in the full consciousness of having loved, but once and to the last and who can say that is not more than a little in a lifetime?

ART WORK
Chattanooga Times (3/13/1880)

Mr. J. H. Moser, the artist, was in the city yesterday, and will remain several days. He has been perfecting some exquisite sketches of points of interest to the artist, tourist and investor, of the scenery along the Alabama Great Southern Railway. These will appear as illustrations of a book to be issued by that enterprising Company at an early date. We have seen some of these works, and know from inspection that the Company did well in securing Mr. Moser's services.

SARAH-ANN

While he was engaged in this work, he left Chattanooga and spent a week in the midst of Tennessee's most picturesque scenery, living in a mountain cabin with natives. While there, he became very friendly with the family which included a teen-age daughter, Sarah-Ann. In the course of his stay he spoke often of his Martha, the subject closest to his heart, and teasing Sarah-Ann in a friendly way, asked her once why she didn't wear shoes. She replied with some spirit, ''I want ye to know Jim, that my feet 'er jes' too tinder fer them things.'' When, upon his leaving, the family were saying their farewells, Sarah-Ann spoke and said, ''Good bye Jim, if'n that 'ar little yankee gal won't have ye, I wul.''

20

J. H. Moser

CABIN, HOT SPRINGS MT. VIRGINIA — 1893

"THE MILKMAID"

With happy youth, and work content,
So sweet and stately on she went.
    Right careless of the untold tale;
Each step she took I loved her more,
And followed to her dairy door
    The maiden with the milking pail.

                  — Jean Ingelow.

21

"THE MILKMAID" — *Painted from life in East Tennessee*   *(Oil — 14 × 11)*   *J. H. Moser*

UNCLE REMUS

HIS SONGS AND HIS SAYINGS

THE FOLK-LORE OF THE OLD PLANTATION

By JOEL CHANDLER HARRIS

*WITH ILLUSTRATIONS BY FREDERICK S. CHURCH AND
JAMES H. MOSER*

NEW YORK
D. APPLETON AND COMPANY
1, 3, AND 5 BOND STREET
1881

22

J. H. Moser

UNCLE REMUS AND LITTLE BOY

Moser met and became quite friendly with Joel Chandler Harris who asked him to make the negro illustrations for his forthcoming book, ''Uncle Remus.''

This commission from Joel Chandler Harris brought James notably before the public, and orders began to roll in from all the prominent magazines of the day: Harper's, Century, Atlantic Monthly and Leslie's Weekly.

OLD PLANTATION PLAY-SONG.

CORN-SHUCKING SONG.

"SEEM LIKE I AIN'T NEVER SEE NO RAW DAY LIKE DAT."

ILLUSTRATIONS FROM UNCLE REMUS by J. H. Moser

THE CHRISTMAS CARD — 1881

In the winter of 1880, the art publishing firm of L. Prang and Co. of Boston, put on a competition for the best Christmas card design, offering a prize of $500. Moser submitted a painting so intricate in design, and with minute detail so perfectly worked out that, though he did not win the prize, in June he received a personal note from Prang.

Atlanta Constitution

"Under the date of June 25th, L. Prang of the famous art publishers of Boston, personally writes as follows in regard to the Christmas card design submitted by Mr. J. H. Moser of this city: 'The more I see of your banner design the more I like it, but the conviction grows with my liking, that it would be next to impossible to reproduce such a mass of minute work as the design consists of. . . . The work does you infinite credit for its conception and execution.' Coming as the above does, from so good an authority as L. Prang, it must be considered as one of the highest compliments that could be paid to anyone."

The design was put in Moser's private collection, and is a treasure still in the hands of the family, although Prang offered later to buy it to cut up and make into a number of small cards.

Moser in his later years in a letter to his friend, Mrs. George Westinghouse, offering "The Christmas Card" for sale said, "It is among the few very valuable examples of my early art and compares favorably with the most notable works in watercolor miniatures. My idea in making it was something that should illustrate Christmas in every land."

24

J. H. Moser

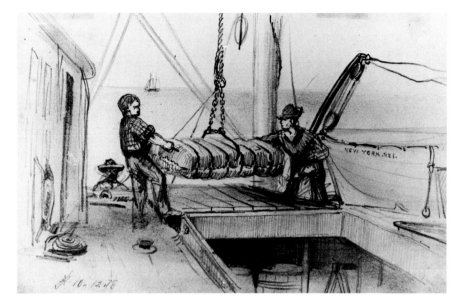

Essex McKann. Atlanta Ga
Model from which
Moser made his
"Uncle Remus"
pictures.

"Remus".

Essex McKann. from life
Moser. 83 - aug 16 - Atlanta Ga

J.H.MOSER.
90

J.H.Moser
to his friend Don Marquis
Dec '05

SKETCHES by J. H. Moser

THE SORGHUM PRESS ON THE OLD PLANTATION

J. H. Moser

On December 26th, 1882, James writes again to his friend Mrs. Hubbard. ''I am on the brink of what seems to me, to promise one of the jolliest times of my artist life. Some time ago Mrs. Banks, wife of a Georgia planter and near relative of our governor, wrote some sketches on the Remus style, describing a little girl's life on a great plantation. She wrote and asked what I would make two sketches for, and I replied that I would make them for $100, to which she assented, saying she would send for me at the depot, Griffin, forty miles from here, and that I should spend the week with herself and family on — yes, on the old plantation! Tomorrow I am to embark (if climbing into the caboose of a freight train can be called embarking) and leave for a romping week on 'The Old Plantation'.''

COUNTRY SING

J. H. Moser

There is no description of this trip, but Mrs. Barnes was so pleased with his illustrations for her book made at that time, asserting that his conception was perfect, and no one in America could have pleased her so well; that two years later she invited him again to be her guest on the plantation, and he spent ten days there making sketches for Frank Leslie's Weekly of negro cabins, scenes and country sings, during a large celebration by several colored societies.

PORTRAIT OF MISS LULA CUNNINGHAM

"Last night the doors of the Art Loan Exhibition were thrown open to the public at the rooms of the Young Men's Christian Association corner of Forsyth and Walton Streets. Under the skillful direction of Mr. James H. Moser, whose labors have been unremitting, the exhibition has taken on a genuinely artistic character, and will prove a most agreeable surprise to all who visit it. Mr. Moser in his untiring devotion to this work has reflected great credit on himself and done great good for art in Atlanta. . . . A gem by Moser is an ideal portrait of Miss Lula Cunningham of this city who posed for the artist and wrote the following verse which is appended to the picture.

"I'm in grandma's dress and just as she stood
With the sunlight aflame in her hair
And I too am waiting the sound of a foot,
(Not grandpa's) upon the stair.''

The Evening Herald. Atlanta.
June, 1882.

In the fall of 1882, Moser became head of the art department in "Miss Ballard's Seminary," thus adding to his already full schedule. As was his wont, he entered enthusiastically into this new work, and by the following winter came this report in the *Atlanta Constitution*. "In Mrs. Ballard's Seminary art rooms an exhibition of pupil's work combined with a loan exhibit was held, which elicited the following from a guest, a former professor from the University of Virginia: 'This exhibition of art is not only a credit to Mr. Moser, the artist, but to the city of Atlanta as well'."

28

GIRL WITH MANDOLIN — 1891

J. H. Moser

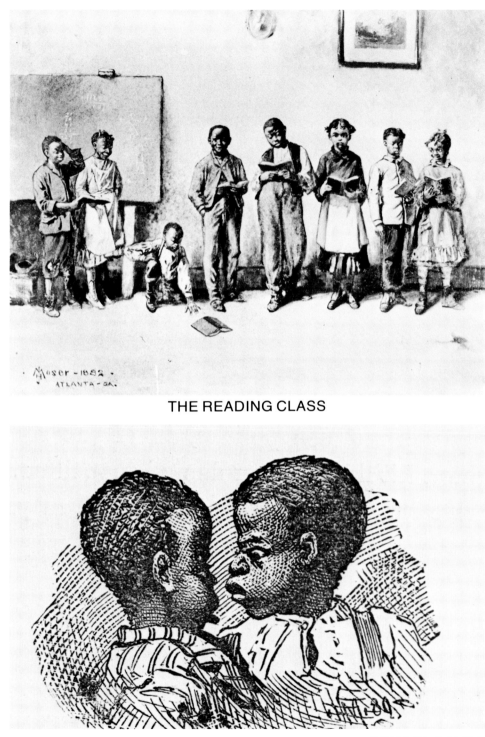

THE READING CLASS

THE ARGUMENT   SCHOOL DAYS by J. H. Moser   THE BOOKWORM

THE WEDDING OF JAMES AND MARTHA

There is a growing demand for art work. . . . Mr. Moser has orders in plenty, and finds no difficulty in selling his carefully finished portraits and landscape pieces. . . . On the eighteenth of this month he marries that nice little yankee girl to whom he has been loyal for seven long years — another Jacob. Good fortune attend them. It is a wish everybody will echo, for genial, gifted, boy-hearted Jimmy Moser has not an enemy in the world.

From "The Literary Casket"
of Franklin, Georgia, October 1883.
"The Sunny South" by Mary E. Bryan.

Yes, James Henry Moser went north to Cornwall, Connecticut, and on October 18th, 1883, married "that little yankee girl," and it was a glorious wedding on one of those golden autumn days for which Connecticut and all of New England are famous.

After a short wedding trip to New York and up the Hudson River by day boat, the young couple returned to Atlanta and passed a happy winter in the large new studio James had secured at 27½ Whitehall Street.

In the spring Martha went to Cornwall, and James followed later for a few months of sketching and painting. From the *Hartford Courant*, August 29: Mr. Moser's vacation work shows great variety, facility and industry. His landscape "Among the Pines" taken from Calhoun's grove, Cornwall, is beautiful and has been purchased by John Calhoun at considerable outlay. The views of Cornwall Lake, the cascade at West Cornwall and his watercolor landscapes and flower pieces are very fine.

30

J. H. Moser

MARTHA SCOVILLE
"THAT LITTLE YANKEE GIRL"

ATLANTA STUDIO — 1883

J. H. Moser

THE STUDIO IN ATLANTA

MARTHA MOSER, northern girl in the south, shared her husband's delight in the quaint ways and language of the colored people. He frequently had a colored boy around the studio to clean up, wash brushes, or if the painting mood was on, to act as model, and from them he acquired a fund of humorous stories which he enjoyed telling, and with which, constantly augmented, he continued to charm audiences through his entire lifetime.

Martha was amused one morning when a colored woman appeared at the door and soberly asked, "White woman, does yu' want a wash lady?"

Once when Old Uncle Essex, model for "Remus" was posing, James who was inordinately fond of his beautiful wife, asked him, "Which is prettier Uncle, my mother or my wife?" The old darkey sat in deep thought a moment, then said in his slow way: "When ol' Missy were young she mus' a bin a blume, but Miss Mattie shore does git 'her now."

Booch, posing for Moser and becoming a little weary, called to his friend Seber who was loafing around the studio, and said: "Take dis year caint an' go t' de g'ocery sto' an' git sumpin' good wid it." Seber took the cent and left, soon to return with a little cornucopia of gray, dried-up prunes. Booch looked at the prunes with disgust and said to Seber, "Aw, w'at d'yu git dem ol' p'unes fer?" "W'at d'yu want ah should git," said Seber. "A b'ack ball." So Seber started out once more. When he returned shortly with one brown cheek sticking out round and shiny, Booch said, "Aw Seba', w'at y' got it in y' mouf fer?" "Well," said Seber reasonably, "Ef'n you gib me a caint t' go t' de g'ocery sto' an' git a b'ack ball wid it, ah guess ah can thuck it on the way home, can't uh?"

One day he was happy and was whistling while he worked. The little colored boy said to him, "Mr. Mosby you must have been a right good whistler a'fore tunes come into fashion." Moser replied, "Wasn't I whistlin' it right?" "No, it goes this a way." The little boy whistled it for him and he could tell the difference.

Dear Moser:

. . . I shall remember the stories that you told at the "Six O'clock Club" till the end of my days. . . .

L. S. Metcalf, Editor of "The Forum."
November 5, 1900.

OLD UNCLE BILL

Oh, I had a fight with Old Satan last night
    as I lay half awake.
He came into my bedroom and a'me began to shake
He shake a'me long; he shake a'me strong;
    he shake a'me clean out a bed.
He carried me to the window and this is what he said.
There's gold in the mountain and silver in the mine.
All these things will be yours Uncle Bill if
    you only will be mine.
Get you gone Old Satan; you come for a'me for to kill.
You can fool some folks with that ere trash,
But you can't fool your old Uncle Bill.
The Lord said, "Well done you good and faithful servant.
"You can sit on my right hand and play on a
    golden harp all day
"Cause you've always been a faithful man."

(Old negro song learned by Moser
and sung by daughter Grace.)

OUR PAPER BOY

J. H. Moser

33

SUPPER TIME

J. H. Moser

AUNT ELLEN

The winter of 1885 James and Martha moved into an apartment of two large, pleasant rooms at number 71½ Peachtree Street and on March 27th a daughter, Grace, was born to them. On June 30th Martha again left for Cornwall with the baby and a colored nurse, and James followed later

The year 1887 found the Mosers in a pleasant little home at 2604 I Street in Washington, D.C. James with his tireless energy was doing pen drawing for the newspapers in addition to his painting. His parents had preceded them there when John was given a position in the Supervising Architect's Office. On July 26th of that year a second daughter, Lydia, was added to the happy family.

By 1889 industry began to pay off and James and his little family were enjoying a comfortable prosperity. They moved early in the year into a larger house, 1519 P Street where he could have his studio at home, and where there was a large yard for the children. They rented one room to an art student, George Dennison, who was working with him, and hired a colored mammy to help with the work and the children. Aunt Ellen was old, had been a slave, and was so wrinkled and homely that Martha wondered at first if she could bear to see her around, but she proved to be so gentle and kindly, loved the children so much and waited on their mother until Martha came to love her too, and said later that there were times when that old black face looked like "an angel's" to her.

James stayed in town late that summer. Letter to Martha, July 30th, 1889. It's five o'clock now and I'm waiting for Aunt Ellen to call me to the "trough." . . . Aunt Ellen is calling. O gee! what a boss dinner, don't know when I've had such an appetite, best meal I've had since you went away. Well, I called for corn pudding this morning, so Aunt Ellen came and set it on the table, and said, "Now don't laf at dis yer puddin', case I ain't neber made none befo'. I was a-studyin' 'bout it dis af'ernoon an' went along up hyar whar a cullud gal serves meals, an' she done tol'me jus' how to make it." Well, it was browned over and incense. There must have been egg, milk, flour, sugar and Lord knows what, but it certainly was delicious. She also had veal chops breaded and fried in egg batter, and they were scrumptuous. This with tea and rye bread was the dinner — yes, and blackberry jam she had made this morning; as she said, "I made dis kase you is allers hollerin' fo' sass. I hope you gwine like it case I put some lem-mon in it." She certainly did, it tasted strong of lemon but I liked it immensely — she made a pint of it. Oh yes, she had beets. I like her dinners better since I kicked against so much "hair oil" in them, she took the hint. Later one day I said, "Aunt Ellen, you are spoiling me for the common cooking I'll have to put up with when my wife gets back," to which she responded with her peculiar "hee-hee." "Yas indeed, shu' de madam can cook, you can' fool me; but you is spoiled — you sut'ny is. Dar neber war no pah' drop' f'um no tree any mo' spoilder dan w'at you is!"

35

J. H. Moser

GRACE MOSER — AGE TWO

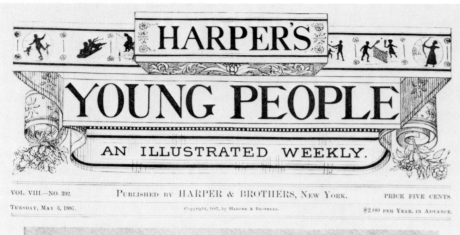

THE WHISTLER   *J. H. Moser*

THE MOONSHINER — 1882 — *Painted from life*   *J. H. Moser*

36

J. H. Moser

J. H. Moser

"COTTON IS KING" — HARPER'S MONTHLY — 1891

38

J. H. MOSER - July '89
Ocean Shore Park - Virginia Beach -
"The Princess Anne" in Distance

"THE PRINCESS ANN" — VIRGINIA BEACH — 1889

J. H. Moser

J. H. Moser

CAPE MAY POINT — LIGHTHOUSE — 1891

White House Notes. From Diary.
December 28, 1889.

Took a portfolio of paintings to the White House for the President and Mrs. Harrison to see. Was invited back in the evening. Called about 7. Was shown into the Red Room where Mrs. Harrison came forward offering her hand in the most friendly way. She introduced Lieut. Parker and his wife (her niece) and Mrs. Dimmick, also a niece. They had the open portfolio on a sofa and were looking at the pictures. We entered into a discussion of them, quite at home. She was enthusiastic and unaffected in her pleasure in watercolor. As I was putting on my coat in the ante room, Lieut. Parker came out and presented me with some orchids, very lovely, which Mrs. Harrison wanted me to take to Mrs. Moser. They were surrounded with delicate ferns. Mrs. Dimmick wore them I had observed. White.

I went from there to Judge Shell with the pictures to leave over Sunday according to promise. I found the Judge in his library. ''What's that?'' said he referring to the flowers. ''Laurels, Judge, laurels,'' I replied. ''Never saw any like 'em.'' ''Well, Judge,'' said I, ''When a young man gives the first private view of his pictures at the White House, and Mrs. Harrison sends orchids to his wife, I think he can be pardoned for calling them laurels!'' ''Yes, young man, yes they are laurels, and you have a right to be very proud of them.''

40

J. H. Moser

Good fortune really broke for James during an exhibition of his paintings held the first two weeks in April at the exclusive art and import galleries of V. G. Fischer on 15th Street. One morning Miss Strickland who lived at the White House, and her friend Miss Kelly, came to the exhibition and in the course of conversation told Mr. Moser that they would like to take lessons from him. Surprised and pleased, he gladly agreed to make the necessary arrangements. Later the President's wife, Mrs. Harrison, came in to the exhibition and bought a picture, ''Morning at Salisbury Beach,'' to hang in the White House.

A SUNNY MORNING AT SALISBURY BEACH   *J. H. Moser*

Lessons at the White House began almost at once and following are excerpts from diary: May. One day too damp for our outdoor sketching, I went alone to Van Ness and sketched the Burns' cottage all but the trees and the sky. I left the drawing at the White House for Miss Strickland to copy while I went for a two-week trip to Cornwall for the apple blossoms, May 14th to June 1st.

J. H. Moser

WHITE HOUSE NOTES

When I returned I called and Miss Strickland handed me a drawing which I thought was my unfinished sketch of Burns' cottage. I started to put it in my portfolio when she said, "But, Mr. Moser, that isn't yours." "What?" said I astonished. "No, that is Mrs. Harrison's copy of your sketch." I could scarcely believe it until I looked closely. Miss Strickland's was not nearly so true and skillful. June 2nd. Mrs. Harrison came down and watched me while I finished the Burns' cottage sketch. Said she would like to become a "scholar." She was sincerely interested. Afterwards I made a watercolor of the view from the south porch of the White House showing monument and river — did it in an hour. While I was at work, Dinsmore brought in six baskets, in a box, of the largest strawberries I ever saw. Mrs. Harrison started to take out a basket and Dinsmore said, "Hadn't I better show them to the President first?" "Oh yes," she said, "and then bring them back." Mrs. Harrison then took one of the finest quart baskets out and put it in my watercolor basket to "take to Mrs. Moser."

The next day she arranged to take Mama, Lillie, Miss Strickland and me out to Piney Branch to take a lesson. This we were unable to do as Miss Strickland came to our house and explained that baby Mary was sick. She is Benjamin McKee's younger sister. That evening before I came away I was introduced to the President who seemed to be the happiest of grandfathers with baby McKee. Mrs. McKee speaks to Mrs. Dimmick of her Uncle Ben, but the baby is always Benjamin.

This afternoon when I came, I was invited up to the hall which is the family living room, and a grand wide room it makes, filled with the most comfortable of furniture, quite luxurious and lovely. It is there that my "Salisbury Beach" hangs, and it looks well, but oh so small beside the huge canvases ten feet square — and some of Bierstadt's very best things. June 13th, another lesson. In the state dining room we hung the orchids, lemon yellow, which were on wire hooks, the orchids having grown to six-inch squares of wood one inch thick, tight like ivy stems. These we hung over a screen by a large south window and went to work. Of all hard things that waxen yellow is the hardest to do! At five I went home and Mattie, Mary (brother George's wife) and I returned to hear the Calvary Band play. The south porch was full of distinguished people. After they had thinned out toward the end of the concert, we went up and were so cordially received — Mrs. Harrison had especially invited us. She introduced us all to the President, invited Mattie to a seat beside her, and I had quite a nice chat with the President — my first of consequence. Mrs. Dimmick invited us in to have lemonade at Mrs. Harrison's suggestion, and altogether we were shown very special attention. Music was fine.

June 16th. I went down and tackled the orchids again this P.M. I almost despair of doing them in watercolor, but am going again tomorrow. Mrs. Harrison is busy packing, but will leave everything to see this experiment through. She painted at it herself, transparently, and got pretty good color, but no texture. She liked my roses and the orange ginger jar still life.

43

FARMHOUSE AND BARN — CAPE MAY POINT

Caroline Scott Harrison

SUMMER AT CAPE MAY POINT

There was a large house built by her grandfather on the farm in Connecticut where Martha was born. This house was vacant, and as Lydia was a delicate child, Martha conceived the idea of living up there for a time in the hope that the higher altitude and fresh air would benefit Lydia. Martha and the children left in May for the farm and James closed the Washington house and joined them in July. He improvised a comfortable studio by putting a high north window in a large upper room in the woodshed and carriage house. Here within a few feet of his family, he worked happily through the summer and fall with the exception of a week at Cape May Point, sketching and continuing his instruction to Mrs. Harrison. When, on one occasion a hard shower drenched the sketching party, James caught a severe cold and sore throat and received the following note from Mrs. Harrison.

"My dear Mr. Moser,

"I am sorry to hear of your cold. We were more fortunate in our ducking. I send paint box and am sorry I have no listerine to send (which is good for sore throat) but we cannot find the bottle. I have gotten my lesson done, but it is not satisfactory to me. The sky is bad, the clouds have sort of a breaking-up look. Will be glad to see you this evening; if you are able, would be glad to see you at supper at six. If however, you do not feel able will be glad to see you later.

Very truly,

Caroline S. Harrison."

November found him in New York and by December he was back in Washington trying to do some business before the New Year.

Excerpts from diary.

Mrs. Harrison, Mrs. McKee, and Mrs. Dimmick met me at the Society in Washington Artists exhibition. I introduced Brooks and Messer. The ladies invited me to lunch at one-thirty. I was there promptly. After a short wait in the Red Room, I was invited into the dining room where the three ladies received me and we enjoyed a pleasant chant before the President arrived. I told them of Ma's praise of the Thanksgiving Proclamation. Mrs. Harrison said, "Those girls put him up to it, urging that the stereotyped form sent down as is the custom from the State Department, ought to be stopped and one with some personal character issued." The President received me cordially, inquiring about Mrs. Moser and the little ones.

The dining room is luxurious in furnishings, but quiet and rich in tone and color. The conversation was easy and cordial. The President's blessing — "Thanks to the Giver of good for those blessings that are always new, make us worthy of them." After lunch the President wished me and mine a happy Christmas and went back to his office. The ladies went into the corridor with me and there presented me with a lovely framed porcelain panel of orchids (10 by 14), and some little flatirons for the children. It was not quite three o'clock when I left.

James returned to Cornwall in time to be with his family for Christmas, and stayed on there with the exception of a trip to New York for the exhibitions; until February when he again went to Washington and held an exhibition of his accumulated work at the Victor G. Fischer's galleries on 15th Street.

44

Caroline Scott Harrison

SAILBOAT OFF CAPE MAY, NEW JERSEY
GIFT TO J. H. MOSER FROM HIS PUPIL CAROLINE SCOTT HARRISON — 1890

Moser said of Mrs. Harrison's talent and interest in art, I regard it as most remarkable when it is remembered that she is an amateur and paints only for recreation. I have had a great many talented pupils, but none with more enthusiasm and genuine love for the art. She is careful and conscientious in all her efforts to render truthfully such subjects as she may happen to fancy. She has shown me watercolors of flowers she had made when she was a girl. She paints flowers on china in almost the highest professional way. Mrs. Harrison has such a distaste for publicity, and is so devoted to her art, that her work is only to be seen to advantage in the beautiful library at the White House which is adorned with many charming examples of her skill.

Letter to Parker Mann. Cornwall, Conn. October 7, 1890.

My eyes were opened to the beauty of the landscape this autumn as never before. I really believe I am approaching that inner Temple where Corot was the great High Priest, and Davis, Wyant, Innis, Tryon, Murphy and Bolton Jones have honored places among the saints. I say it reverently that I am getting close to nature where she reveals herself as supreme art. Undoubtedly, the best art is a direct inspiration from nature and comes not from the personality of the artist. I have sometimes thought the artist's individuality and genius was the supreme thing, but I feel quite sure his genius is that of discernment of beauty that exists by God's Grace in nature, but is a sealed book to those who are not gifted with this second sight. My own experience has been that hitherto the brilliant, dazzling yellows, reds, purples, and blues of autumn quite turned my head. I remember my past ecstacy over these gay effects in nature, but this year, though I have not denied their beauty — at eve and sunrise I have found a more wonderful tenderness and harmony — a color so ravishing that my color-sense has thrilled to a pitch I never dreamed of. And how hard I have studied, for these beauties are elusive and must be dug out.

Eve after eve I have leaned on the stone wall down by the brook where a great variety of meadows, woods, rocky ledge, and distant, low-lying mountains spread on all sides and the lake at my back. I have caught pleasing combinations of color, and the more earnestly I followed them the more beauty developed, like a negative in which the image comes up more distinctly while you watch it in the bath. These sunset glows and the nature and color of the trees against the sky were something very lovely, but the thing that nearly flattened me out was the pale yellow moonrise at sunset. Davis or Wyant might paint it, but I'm sure they never have just as I have seen it evening after evening — for sunset and moonrise came close together for some days. I have seen in Cazin fine suggestions of such a moment, and in Davis's Waggaman picture there was a poetry and sentiment sweet and, at the same time, a majesty about the composition that was all but bewildering. I shall try to paint it and feel certain of some measure of success, for I am so deeply impressed with that effect. My sketchbooks are teeming with beautiful motives and elaborate notes on color, etc. Next winter will not be half long enough to do the things I've planned. Coming home last of the month. This is but escaping steam Ol' man, obliged to tell somebody or biler'd bust. . . . Jim.

47

SPRING EVENING

J. H. Moser

KILLING OF THE BUFFALO — 1888
Two handsome pictures for the National Museum.

Two pictures which attracted must attention at the exposition in Cincinnati will in a few days grace the walls of the national museum, for which institution they were painted. They are the work of a Washington artist, Mr. J. H. Moser, and are companion pieces. The first, ''The Deadly Still-Hunt,'' showing the western plains thickly spotted with large herds of buffalo, hunter prostrate on a ledge at the right is in itself a complete history and tells more eloquently than words the ruthless way in which 5,000,000 buffaloes were slaughtered in five years for the sake of their pelts. One who views this picture can readily account for the almost total extinction of this valuable beast. What might be termed the sequel to the story is entitled, ''Where the Millions Have Gone,'' and is a fitting finale to the first. The bleaching bones of thousands of carcasses dotting the verdant plains of Montana are silent monuments of the wanton destruction carried on from 1871 to 1875, and which was not at that time considered of any consequence, but is now fully appreciated, particularly in the far west. The artist, whose only ground to work on was from information furnished by Mr. W. T. Hornaday and photographs of the country, has handled his subjects in a masterly manner, and people familiar with the scenes say they could not be more accurate in any particular.

In the winter of 1890 Moser was given a commission to paint two large murals (canvases 50 by 28 feet) from the same pictures for the Smithsonian Institute, to cover completely the two ends of the Indian exhibit room.

NOTE: These pictures are probably one of the earliest attempts to educate the public to the need for the conservation of wildlife. The two oil paintings, 45" by 61", are now in possession of the Jefferson National Expansion Memorial, St. Louis, Missouri.

48

J. H. Moser

49

THE BUFFALO STUDY *(Oil — 10 × 14)*

J. H. Moser

THE DEADLY STILL-HUNT   *(Oil — 45 × 61)*

J. H. Moser

51

WHERE THE MILLIONS HAVE GONE   *(Oil — 45 × 61)*

J. H. Moser

THE BLOUNTS

During the early years in Washington the Mosers became lifelong and devoted friends of Mr. and Mrs. Henry F. Blount of "The Oaks," later known as Dumbarton Oaks in Georgetown.

The friendship began when Moser painted a series of portraits, heads in pastel from photographs, of their beautiful teenage daughter who had just died of scarlet fever. The portraits were so skillfully and sympathetically done that the Blounts were more than pleased; and as they came to know him, his sunny good humor and gentle wit so captivated them that from that time on, figuratively speaking, their latch-string was always out to him and his family. They had two daughters, young ladies and two young sons.

To Martha. May 20, 1892.

Just in from the Blounts. I made a sketch of Mary in her empire dress. My experience with figures for the magazines has given me considerable facility in that line, and these sketches will help greatly my collection for next fall and winter. I am going to pack up and enjoy a week's good solid work there after I am all done in town. That is the only way out; otherwise, they will be offended for they have been so persistent in their invitation to make them a visit while I am here alone. I have an order from the Glen Echo people for twelve small watercolors which I shall stay on to do.

In the year of the great World's Fair in Chicago, 1893, James Henry Moser had three pictures on exhibition in the Fine Arts Building with the consequence that he had a season pass to the grounds. He spent two months out there living student fashion with an accomplished amateur, Mr. McCombs of St. Louis. Of this time he wrote later, "I count that charming summer the most important study period of my life."

52

J. H. Moser

53

J. H. Moser

LAKE SCENE WITH BOATS — 1893

"MARTHA'S ALBUM"

From the day James proposed marriage to Martha on June 23rd, 1877, he cherished that golden day and always sent or gave her some token of remembrance; at first small pictures sent in letters, later perhaps a book or bit of jewelry. On June 23rd, 1892, his gift was a beautiful leather-bound album bearing in gilt letters on its cover "To My Wife, Martha Scoville Moser. June 23, 1892." This book was partially filled with the tiny paintings and sketches he had sent to her during the long seven years of his courtship and waiting, and those he had given or sent to her during the time since; each small picture with a cherished memory behind it for these two who found love through their art.

54

"To My Wife, Martha Scoville Moser. June 23, 1892."

"To June"

Month of the perfect love
Month of the perfect leaf.

"Song"

Do the mountains query;
   Whence our beauteous trees?
Do the waves make question
   The glory of the seas?
Do the skies insist on
   The stars' bright mystery?
Shall I seek to fathom
   The love I bear to Thee?

George H. Hillman
Harper's June, 1900.

J. H. Moser

"GRACE AND LYDIA" — PLAYING SUNDAY SCHOOL — 1890

55

MARTHA MOSER — JUNE 23, 1892

J. H. Moser

56

GRACE

J. H. Moser

Berlin, Germany
June 23, 1896

My Dear,

This morning was so dark and rainy, I was homesick. I caught sight of a pretty bouquet of roses that were beginning to wilt. The landlord's daughter had gotten them for me and they were so beautiful in their last hours, a few petals scattered on the stand cover, the photo of you and the children leaning against a blue glass candlestick, I sat admiring them and thinking of home when it occurred to me, why not paint it for Mama's album as a souvenir of June 23rd? My homesickness vanished. I got my things and just settled down to do my level best, regardless of time.

I put your last letter behind a candlestick to get all the sentiment into it, and made a picture. Well, I was nearly from nine till three doing it, and positively, as it grew true under my hand, I was in perfect delight — so happy I could scarcely be happier if I were home, for I knew what pleasure it would give you to get such a little study. It would make you think of the old loving days that were not so sweet as present days — no, no more than the old-time pictures are not nearly so good as this. If I were only there to receive the thank-you kiss, and hear your voice.

Your own Jim.

J. H. Moser

"GERMAN ROSES" FOR MAMA

Martha Scoville Moser
James Henry Moser

To the Sweetest Girl
    The Jolliest Companion
    The Sensible Woman
    The ''Beautiful'' Mama,
To the most loyal, unselfish and
    Devoted Wife

    From Her
        Husband

who after nearly ten years of married ''ups'' and ''downs'' is quite sure he finds in her the ''Dream'' of his early manhood fulfilled.

● ● ● ●

''You are a great little wife, and I don't know what I would do without you.'' And as he spoke, he put his arms about her and kissed her, and she forgot all the cares in that moment. And forgetting all, she sang as she washed the dishes, and sang on as she made the beds, and the song was heard next door; and a woman there caught the refrain also, and the two homes were happier because he had told her that sweet old story — the story of the love of a husband for a wife. . . .'' Anonymous.

58

GRACE HOLDING LYDIA   *J. H. Moser*

HOME IN ATLANTA   *J. H. Moser*

59

LYDIA   MOSER'S DAUGHTERS   GRACE

J. H. Moser

STEPHEN CRANE AS A PAINTER KNEW HIM
by
JAMES HENRY MOSER — 1895

My cousin Fred Gordon, an artist and illustrator, sent me a copy of ''Maggie'' with a note asking what I thought of it, and adding simply, ''You will see Crane when you come to New York for he is stopping in the studio with me. He is a genius.'' Though a bald affair with bare brick walls and smoky cobwebbed rafters high overhead, the studio was an immense room in size and attractiveness to a worker. The skylight itself was the largest in New York in the studio of an individual painter, for it had been the life Class Room in those days when ''The Art Student's League'' occupied the Needham Building on Twenty-third Street.

''Maggie'' shocked and fascinated me, for here was held to ugly nature an honest mirror singularly clear and uncompromising. Beyond that, there shone through the story that silver thread of genius which gleamed in the simplicity, the disguised art and the subtle interpretation. It was that class of literature where painter quality dominates the abstract as well as the concrete atmosphere, and it seemed to me to be crisp and graphic as anything of Zola, Kipling or Sargent.

Soon after this time there appeared in ''The Press'' a review of Crane's ''Maggie'' by Mr. Howells which, if I remember rightly, declared this little work of fiction to be the greatest novel or study of American life that had so far appeared.

I was surprised to find, on meeting Crane in New York, that he was a mere slip of a smooth-faced boy — a most conventional young bohemian, steeped in tobacco smoke. His clothes were shabby, like the run of students and struggling hand-to-mouth young artists that swarm about the old studio buildings in New York. There was always in his well worn dress at this time some article of apparel ultra-fashionable in character betraying the true penniless bohemian disposition to ape the swell on occasion. Your true bohemian hates this swell most earnestly, but it is like an occasional flawless spree when the spirit moves. Nothing is too ''correct'' for him when he launches out with a determination to dress ''up to date.'' He despised anything which savored of prudence, or a desire to husband strength, or preserve one's health. When rebuked for his recklessness and reminded, as he often was, that he was the only genius in the company, and that we felt that he ought to take care of himself, he would, without removing his pipe, reply — ''Rot, you guys make me weary. I expect to get done by the time I'm thirty-five and I'll last that long allright.''

In those studio days when we were practicing the nicest economy and the careful, methodical Gordon was father and mother to us, Crane spent his nights roaming the slums to gather material for his books and slept in the daytime on one of the two cot beds which Gordon and I occupied at night. He drifted in and out of the studio with the freedom of a wayward, but dearly beloved child; jolly, joking, story-telling and singing snatches of the most rollicking Bowery songs, ''The Prod's Return'' being a great favorite with him. This lad had, as true painters do, enjoyment in his art for its own sake. Hints of fame and recognition which came fitfully in press paragraphs and fine letters from discerning editors, seemed to mean nothing to him beyond the fact that they were evidence that he was a step nearer the goal of his ambition, which was to show those guys real art.

THE PROD'S RETURN

There was an old man and he had two sons
    he had, he had
He lived on a ranch so the story runs
    he did, he did
It was built on the beautiful Queen Anne plan
    right next to the New Jerusalem
The vicinity it don't matter a damn
    sing tra la la, la la.

The elder son was a goodly man
    he was, he was
He was built on the Moody and Sanky plan
    he was, he was
With a sweet and sanctimonious face
    he talked about love and undying grace
And he wanted a seat in the heavenly place
    sing tra la la, la la.

But the younger son was a son of a gun
    he was, he was
He shuffled the cards and he played for mon
    he did, he did
He wore a silk hat and a high standing collar
He'd go out with the boys, get full
    then he'd holler
Oh, he was one Jim dandy loller
    sing tra la la, la la.

The old man's purse was long and fat
    it was, it was
The Prod he was right on to that
    he was, he was
And he of the sanctimonious smile
Kept his weather eye right onto the pile
And he hoped he'd get there after a while
    sing tra la la, la la.

To divide on the square the old man did his best
    he did, he did
The Prod took his share and lit out for the West
    he did, he did
Fell in with some cowboys and had a great time
Woke up in the morning with nary a dime
Stranded way out in a foreign clime
    sing tra la la, la la.

A telegraph man in his office sat
    out west, out west
When in ran a man without any hat
    or coat, or vest
Come, send this message right over the track
The Prod is a wreck and he's coming back
Have plenty of veal for one on the rack
    sing tra la la, la la.

The answer he got was both short and direct
    it was, it was
It said yours received, go to blazes, collect!
    it did, it did
But the Prod was used to those knock-downs of fate
He pawned his suspenders and went on a skate
And started for home on a limited freight
    sing tra la la, la la.

To a lawyers office he went next day,
    he did, he did
He sued the old folks for pay while away
    he did, he did
Got out an injunction and put them all out
Oh, he was a lolla you hear me shout
That's the kind of a Prod I'm singing about
    sing tra la la, la la.

Now this is as far as the story goes
    it is, it is
What the end of it is I think nobody knows
    not one, not one.
    sing tra la la, la la.

STEPHEN CRANE

Guys was a favorite word with him at this time and in this instance referred to that well fed brood of popular, but superficial writers of fiction, and Philistine editors whom he hated cordially.

Mr. Hamlin Garland, to whom more than anyone else perhaps, the world is indebted for Crane because of his discovery and subsequent kindness to the young writer, has published a comprehensive account of young Crane's experiences. In that story is an account of the five or six art students 'Indians'' Crane called them, with whom he lived in a room below Gordon's studio. This was before Crane left the Indians and went to live with Gordon. They were a noisy, thriftless lot, but their lives and characters were an open book. They had nothing to conceal from each other and Crane, while seeming a part of it, watched them greedily and pictured them truly in ''The Third Violet.'' Every waking moment he was an observer and student when there was anything to be studied; when there was not, he abandoned himself to hilarious, non-sensical songs and the wittiest Bowery chaff.

I once spoke of the novel, artistic quality of his work reminding me of the truth and simplicity of Bret Harte's earlier stories, and asked him how he liked them, to which he replied, ''I never read any of em, why, I haven't read anything. I'm reading Rousseaus 'Confessions' now, Mr. Howells told me to read it. It's a cussed big book and dry, but there's some great stuff in it — some great stuff.'' It was curious, Crane's small acquaintance with books. When I related the story of ''Tennessee's Partner'' to him, and quoted some passages from it, he said, ''Fine, I'm sure I'd like that.''

Crane shared our enthusiastic admiration of the work of Kipling, Howells and Garland. When he began

to do ''The Black Riders'' and read some of them to us, Gordon and I looked at each other in amazement. It was such a far away flight from ''Maggie'' and ''The Red Badge of Courage'' since they were done in free verse. When he brought home the manuscript of ''George's Mother,'' a story scarcely second to ''Maggie'' in subject matter, I read his original manuscript while he corrected the typewritten copy. I remember saying how impossible it would be to make illustrations for that work, for every reader who knew such characters and the local color, would have so vivid a picture of George and his mother, that any illustration, even photographs of Crane's living models — if he had any — would seem foreign to the story. Crane agreed with me fully, remarking that most illustrations to stories were independent rivals of the text.

Crane would insist that the moral purpose of his art was rather to turn the searchlight upon evil than in preaching about those evils. The moral, he thought, should be obvious enough to all serious minded people who had any interest in the welfare of the race. That man was his brother's keeper, Crane was sure, and his most vindictive and brilliant tirades were always directed against those smug selfish Pharisees who talk about their sympathy for the unfortunate, but never try to mend things at short range. Crane's special aversion was Y.M.C.A. people. Had he known them as intimately as he knew his East side characters he would have felt differently, for at heart Crane revered Christ's personality and teachings, but he never knew well a man like McBurney of blessed memory, and it was a great pity. The fault was his own — his antagonism widened the gulf, and he never knew the sterling stuff of which the Y.M.C.A. is made, and the good work it is accomplishing among struggling young men.

It is not for a painter, whom wise John Lafarge says "should keep out of the literary field," to undertake an analysis, or even a review of Crane. and his work, but this much I may be permitted to venture. Goethe said, "Fortunate is he who in his youth knows true art," and of all the painters or writers I have ever known in their youth, Crane more than any other knew art instinctively. He had the clearest vision and seemed to have had it by inspiration in the very beginning. I know nowhere of a sentence that so exquisitely describes a subtle and momentary aspect of nature which few, but landscape painters with that schooled inner sensitiveness of eyesight perceive, as this particular one of Crane's: "The little white birches make a melody in the silence," and his work abounds in such artistic strokes. Crane has been ranked with Kipling and Poe. "The Open Boat" and "The Black Riders" support that claim. However, that is a question of small consequence now, and one that the critics of the coming century may settle among themselves. It is enough to know that he was a true artist, honest, fearless — and that he was, at heart, thoroughly wholesome and happy throughout his all too short life, and this can be said of few geniuses.

I received a letter from Crane from Galveston when he was on his way to Mexico, but have seen nothing of him after the publication of 'The Black Riders" and the fine prosperity which immediately followed. I also made a sketch of him in Gordon's studio when he was at work on "George's Mother." The only comment he made upon it was, "Say, Jimmie, that's all right."

When I was leaving New York Crane produced a copy of "Maggie: A Girl of the Streets" on the fly-leaf of which he wrote this fanciful inscription: "To Jim Moser from Stephen Crane. May his smile blossom like an electric light for many years. May his genial words string together like amber beads for many more years, and may he not die before he gets good and ready." Gordon's studio, New York.

J. H. Moser

MURALS FOR THE BOLKENHAYN HOTEL

The country was going through a depression during the years of the second Cleveland administration. Artists, who were always first to feel the squeeze, were selling little. James was fortunate in having the comfortable home in Cornwall where his family was safely away from the distress felt in the big cities. He was producing fine work, but the art exhibitions brought in little and his other efforts in New York and Washington seemed equally fruitless. His brother-in-law, Alfred Zucker, now remarried and living in New York, had been trying to get him to establish a permanent studio there. In the fall of 1894 he got him a commission to paint the murals for a large apartment hotel he, Alfred, was constructing. These Moser painted in the Cornwall studio in the winter of 1894 and 1895 and the hotel was opened in April.

November 28, 1895. Boston, Mass. Special to the Washington Post.

James Henry Moser of Washington is one of the artists who succeeded in getting work hung at the Second Annual Exhibition of the exclusive Copley Society, in progress here. The Copley Society is Boston's chief art association and one of the most noted in America. The strictness of the judges can be understood from the more than eight hundred rejections. The present exhibition is one of the finest the Society has ever given.

THE LITTLE ARTIST

J. H. Moser

65

J.H. Moser

86TH STREET, WESTSIDE, NEW YORK — 1892

THE EUROPEAN TRIP

Moser made a trip abroad in the summer of 1896 which lasted three months. It came about when Alfred Zucker invited him to accompany him to Freiburg, Germany, to paint portraits of his aging father and mother whom he had not seen in ten years. They sailed together on the thirteenth of June.

Landing in Southampton, they stopped briefly in London before taking a night boat from New Haven to Dieppe, thence to Paris where they spent a day before going on to Berlin. Here Alfred left James to spend a few days while he hastened on to his home and parents in Freiburg. Alfred's parents appeared however, so much older than he had anticipated, that he decided not to have the portraits painted, wishing rather to remember them as he had known them. This left Moser free to paint whatever he chose during the three months he had planned to stay.

The little town of Bolkenhain, not far from Freiburg where Alfred had taken him before he left, so charmed James that he took a room there and spent six weeks painting the old castle, quaint houses, churches and flower gardens. He made thirty medium-sized watercolors and many small sketchbook sized ones which he pencilled in "on the spot" and colored nights in his room. These small sketches he continued to make during his whole trip with a series of descriptive letters to accompany them. Leaving Bolkenhain August 11th he went to Dresden for a short visit, continued on to Hamburg, then to Southampton. After spending time in England he went back to Paris with a short stop in Amsterdam and sailed for New York on the "Spree" September 9th.

Freiburg, Germany. July 7, 1896.

My Dear: I shall be brief in these descriptive letters and only touch on the things that strike me particularly. John Burroughs, on his first trip to England — it was in June, said nothing impressed him so much as the greenness of the grass. That I felt too, and think it due to the weedlessness and park-like condition of cultivation.

The English houses are of Victorian Gothic, the modern ones not pleasant, but the old ones are very picturesque. The low thorn hedges so carefully nurtured, have all their holes mended with basketwork, and of such are the gates — very light. I missed big trees and barbed-wire fences.

The factory houses, so poor and such swamps of them just alike, are so unkempt and suggestive of slavery. The approach to London is like New York, so gradual you hardly know it till you find yourself on an elevated track looking down on a vast sea of smokey housetops with chimney pots as thick as stubble in a stubble-field.

Dieppe with its old French houses and church all alone on a high cliff overlooking the sea, was beautiful in the early morning light; but words cannot convey the beauty of the little sylvan valley we followed that morning just before sunrise (we had reached Dieppe at 3:30 A.M.). The greens were so delicate and silvery, the cows were picture cows, clean and sweet in perfect harmony with the landscape; the quaint houses were so snug and cosy behind garden walls, and so every which way — picturesque to the last degree.

"I dreamt that I dwelt in m. h. etc —"

Hotel Cecil Thames Embankment Aug

J. H. Moser

BAND CONCERT — HOTEL CECIL — LONDON — 1896

A LITTLE GERMAN TOWN
by
JAMES HENRY MOSER

Bolkenhain is a quaint little German village with steep irregular streets leading up to a wonderful old ruined castle. A market square, a City Hall, two churches and a few shops. The houses, most of them, are small and very old. The castle wall that once enclosed the town appears here and there grown in with the later generation of homes, surrounded by flower gardens and many trees. Towards evening, and on cloudy days, the little town presents such a succession of charming velvety pictures that to me, a stranger within its gates unused to anything not American, it seemed a dream town.

Excepting a few phrases I had learned en route, I knew nothing of German and so had that exquisite pleasure one fancies a deaf and dumb person must experience in the presence of beautiful things.

I am still wondering what that good-natured porter at the Hotel of the Black Eagle thought of me as I hurried with him from one vacant room to another, paying no attention whatever to the room and its conveniences, looking only out of the windows for views; finally, but not without difficulty, making him understand that number 16 was the room I wished and that the price was satisfactory. From my window, only a few hundred yards away, the castle stood out solitary and sphinx-like against the western sky. This window also looked out upon the market square with its fountain and peace monument. To the right stood the yellow, stuccoed City Hall with a typical spire green from oxidized copper. On the left rose the simple round clock tower of the oldest of the two churches.

On the Hotel side of the square, fortunately for my view, were the modern commercial structures and conventional sidewalk. Across the square, opposite, the houses were very old, standing shoulder to shoulder. Three stories and about the same height, but with such variation in design as to make a most picturesque arrangement and fine sky line. All stucco surfaces whitewashed, blue, pink, yellow and green washed in delicate tints. All weather stained into a harmony I found infinite pleasure in studying on rainy days. To these houses or stores huge stone steps led from the street without sidewalk to a succession of heavy round arches of the high arcade that extended a distance of three city blocks upon that side of the street.

Here was a German town teeming with paintable things at my very door — as entirely new to the world of art as it was unfamiliar to me. I was all on fire. A painter will understand the delicious sensation, how the blood thrills in the presence of material new and exactly to ones liking.

Lamenting that it was too late in the afternoon to unpack my water color box, I hastened out for an evening stroll, being a true sundowner, for rain or shine, the world seems the most beautiful at this time. Yes, to him who hath eyes to see, the fairies are ever dancing in the landscape at sundown. Going in the direction of the castle, for that promised the most comprehensive view of my new "find," I ascended by a winding path, "footways," the Germans call them. They are usually short cuts from the main road. No picturesque spot, no fine point of view is without its perfectly kept "foot-way." Of the many delightful memories one returns with, none are more lasting and deeply enjoyed than those rambles along winding foot-ways.

68

J. H. Moser

MARKET SQUARE — BOLKENHAIN

Arriving at the summit, just northward of the castle I found a rustic bench facing the sunset and that repose which is said to lie on every height. A serene July evening. A large part of the town was already in the blue shadow of the Bolkoburg tower. The castle is now a roofless ruin standing upon the summit of the highest hill in the neighborhood, about 500 feet above the valley through which a little stream runs. Beyond, far to the southward, lie the Risengebirge Mountains. Northward and westward fall away the rolling hills of houseless and fenceless fields under perfect cultivation. These fields, so long and narrow, look like ribbons of every delicate shade of green and yellow with an occasional strip of purple gray plowed ground.

From my bench the view was expansive and restful, but paintable? — Well, as some Frenchman once said, ''It may be so, but before God it is impossible.'' The glimpses one gets of ''bits to paint'' are so numerous as to make the sketchbook heavy with rough gems that are, alas, too often never cut.

Eastward from the castle the descent is more gradual and it is upon this side that the little town is located. Of the great variety of houses, as to material and architecture in Bolkenhain, I found those most interesting that were of brick, plastered and whitewashed. The latter process repeated so frequently that they always look thoroughly wholesome. These white walls take such fascinating tones in shadow and on cloudy days; the old-fashioned flowers and vines have a lovely effect in relief against them. Particularly the rose trees which in themselves are lovely beyond the power of words to describe. People cannot be unhappy who cherish flowers as the Germans do. Their flowers grow luxuriantly — not one half-dead or thriftless plant to be found anywhere.

Windows brimming full and little gardens of astonishing smallness, enclosed by frail picket fences made to keep out nothing stronger than a hen. These little enclosures are marvels of color which I found it impossible to paint satisfactorily. Nevertheless, I am impatient for the return of another opportunity to ''try my hand'' on ''the most beautiful things God ever made and forgot to put a soul into.''

All over Germany one sees houses with exposed timber construction in with the white plaster surface. The logs are hewn and plastered between the joints presenting a fairly smooth surface. The stables and sheds, generally attached to the houses, are so interwoven with them that where one begins and the other ends is difficult to determine. Moss of the tenderest green often covers the lumpy decayed thatch or red tile, and brings the buildings into close harmony with the surrounding trees just as moss does some fallen tree or rock in the woods at home.

So much in Bolkenhain is odd and unusual that one is continually wondering ''why?'' only to be met by the answer that it all goes back so far nobody knows.

The sun had just disappeared below the horizon, a slender crescent in a pale yellow sky with a flush of rose in the smoky tones — one of those skies that always seem quite enough for one canvas. The crescent grew brighter till it became the only detail in the landscape. Darkness was close upon me. I retraced my steps to the hotel filled with good resolutions for work. Things one has longed for a lifetime to see are often so disappointing while unheard of places prove a revelation and charm beyond words to express. This was true of Bolkenhain where I went to sketch for a couple of days and spent the busiest six weeks I ever knew.

STREET SWEEPER — BOLKENHAIN

J. H. Moser

Bolkenhain. July 18.

How time flies! These poor notes will never get written I fear if I don't leave my sketching stool before 8:15 P.M. as I did tonight. I got a sketch of a typical German house today, many hundreds of years old, with its black rafters showing against a white-washed field.

I tell you what, you don't know what friendliness is till you come to Germany, and everybody so. No dogs and sinister faces. Everyone greets you with a ''guten tag,'' ''g'uten morgen,'' or ''g'abend.'' The boys, most of them, lift their hats with a grand sweep, many of the men also; and everybody greets you cordially.

There is a watchmaker across the street from me here, Alfred Lahrmer, a fine athletic fellow who was in America six years and speaks very good English. We took a walk to Wormsdorf the other evening just as the sun was setting over the western hills. Fine sunset, as we walked up the hill along a path through a field of waving grain we could see the noble outline of the Bolkoburg against the sunset sky and the salmon-colored wafer of the moon above it. There was the faint line of mountains beyond and the veritable checkerboard landscape without fences or houses one sees around here.

Coming down the hill we came upon one of those farm establishments called a ''Dominion,'' a great square surrounded by walled barns of inconceivable size and stoutness. At the gasthaus of ''The White Lamb,'' we went in and got a glass of beer, 1¼ cents. Quaint, coarse, primitive place, and such a rowdy, Sunday-night crowd, low drawling peasants, but good humored. Beautiful walk back with the moonlight through the trees, and lights in the odd little windows.

Bolkoburg Castle.

Here I write down some of the things I have been able to find out about the old castle which is one of the oldest and most primitive structures in Europe. It stands on a steep hill overooking a broad expanse of rolling valley, with a sharp cliff on one side. The original wall extended from the castle on the easterly side and surrounded the town. The size and strength of the castle are enormous. It pleases me because it is so vast and, at the same time, so primitive architecturally. Wall after wall seventy-five feet and higher surround the main house. The whole covers 50 metres and the first mention of it in German history is in 1276, although the ''Turm'' (tower) which is the oldest portion dates back to 800 A.D. In shape it seems to be round until you come near to it on the flattened sides, and it is said to be as deep in its cellar as it is above ground though that seems impossible. The walls of the main building are eight feet thick and I saw rooms not over twelve feet square with window openings eight feet deep. Since Prussia took possession of the Borg in 1810 no one has lived there. The state holds it.

This town has scarcely two hundred houses and nestles so closely and picturesquely at the foot of the Borg that gardens the second block from this hotel which is on market square, the center of town, are at the foot of the wall.

73

H MOSER - 1896 -

BOLKOBURG CASTLE

J. H. Moser

The milk wagon in Berlin is white with five faucets along the side for different kinds of milk. The milkman has a key with which he turns the faucet, and boys, dressed in smocks, sitting on the end of the wagon carry the milk into the houses, much of it in quart and pint bottles with patent stoppers much like ours.

I have never seen dogs work the way they do in this country. They tug and pull as faithfully as horses, sometimes harnessed together, sometimes single, and the stout little wagons look so heavy. The harness is elaborate and often tailormade with highly polished brass trimmings. I saw a boy sitting in front driving along the road with a good big wagon load of hay and an old woman on behind with a rake.

In Potsdam I saw dwarf apple trees, three feet, some only two feet, with finely developed apples just like a big tree.

I am so homesick for my dear little daughters and hope they are enjoying these letters.

Bolkenhain. July 30, 1896.

My Dear: Up at four A.M. yesterday by the alarm clock. Lahrmer had breakfast with me and we took a 5:13 train for Breslau, 4th class. This is like a baggage car with a bench a foot wide running around it. Of the fifteen people on the train, fourteen were fourth class; well dressed, people down to bare-footed peasants. At Strigow the car became crowded with women carrying big baskets of butter and farm produce to Breslau. Such a crowd of women and children and baggage from the size of a trunk down. Three hours to go thirty miles on a hard bench in extreme heat! The people were good natured and did not seem to mind the thick tobacco smoke and bad air but, I had to get my face to one of the tiny windows.

The Oder River runs through the town and on its banks are beautiful parks full of folks, and I never saw so many babies. The streets are fine and there are some wonderful old houses. The "Rathhaus" is the most beautiful bit of architecture I've seen so far. This is architecture of the quaintest kind of German Gothic, red and green tiles, not church-like.

I sketched an odd little church that was built in 1460. It was the hottest day I ever went sightseeing; we sweltered, and cool places could only be found in beer kellars, and they smelled bad. On the way back the car as far as Strigow was jammed with the same conglomerate crowd as when we went, only some were so sleepy and some were so drunk — but good natured as ever. They were munching sausage, bread and cheese, and such cheese! The air was oppressive enough without it. It will be a long time before I relish cheese again.

75

H.MOSER-1896-

J. H. Moser

MARKET — BOLKENHAIN

Bolkenhain. August 4.

Work went fine today though I was very tired tonight from a full day's work in the open air, and stiff from sitting so long. I have a new scheme; I send my boy into a neighboring house for a chair when my camp stool becomes unbearable. Today he brought me a heavy, broad, polished mahogany chair out of a house from whose outward appearance you'd suppose they sat only on kegs and soap boxes. The broad seat was flat as any table — the change was such a relief! This kid next door, Kurt, a lad of nine years, goes with me all day for 2½ cents, and half a day for 1½ cents. School is out now and they all flock around me and want to go. The price seems ridiculous, and I have no need for a boy my kit is so light and everything so close by, but I enjoy his company, and seeing his eyes sparkle when the 5 pfennigs drops into his hands. I tell you small change is scarce among youngsters here. I painted a boy's portrait yesterday P.M. while it rained, three hours; gave him 20 pf, 5 cents, and he came around this P.M. while I was at work, bragging to the other youngsters about the "big money" he had made yesterday in only three hours. I could understand enough to see they all regarded it with as much awe as a man feels who draws a big sum in a lottery.

76

August 6.

This morning I painted an old house and this P.M. a curious little garden full of hollyhocks. The hollyhocks were so lovely, and the background of hillside so fine with a piece of the Borg wall, I worked till I could no longer see — cloudy, and it was half past seven when I quit.

J. H. Moser

LITTLE GERMAN BOY

J. H. Moser

STREET SCENE — BOLKENHAIN

DRESDEN, SAXONY.
August 11.

My Dear: Finished my work Saturday, and Sunday and by Monday I was so impatient for this morning to come was up at four-thirty to see the weather — opened up clear and beautiful. Last night I had every sock of my "socken" packed, but it was after midnight when I turned in. Early this morning I gave the little watercolors to five friends — those to Proprietor Triebe's girls here at the hotel were perhaps, the most appreciated. When I said good-bye to dear mama Triebe — she must weigh three hundred, and is scarcely fifty, she hugged and kissed me till I was almost embarrassed; dear soul, tears stood in her eyes and rolled down her cheeks. That hugging was a curious sensation. It felt like lying on one of these German feather beds! Dear, good, motherly soul couldn't understand a word of English and I was not up in German terms of affection, so could only "take it."

Lahrmer and his two little girl cousins went with me to Merzdorf twelve miles, where I took the train, and with all my luggage it made a big load. Charge 3 marks, 75 cents — that is not only cheap German rates, that is friendship. The air was clear, and on the train I was surprised to find we passed through mountain scenery like the White Mountains, some beautiful views.

Arrived here at five and took a cab to "Hospiz Zinzendorf-Strasse" which Triebe recommended. It is new and altogether the handsomest hotel I have seen in Europe. Was most surprised when, as Triebe said, I found I could get a room for sixty cents a night.

August 12.

Was at the great National Gallery of pictures this morning from ten till two-thirty, and it is great and no mistake. Wandered about later until it began to rain, then I went into a cafe where I heard they had papers. Bought a Paris edition of the New York Tribune and a cup of coffee. How behind I am with the news!

Walked out for a stroll this evening to "Old Market Square." I was charmed with the picturesque architecture. This is a wonderful city, words cannot describe it and photos, but poorly.

SISTINE MADONNA ROOM.
10:30 A.M.

Good soft light — not entirely clear outside. Wandered through a labyrinth of old masters, before I found it in the north end in a room twenty by fifty and quite twenty feet high.

The painting looks small, figures about life size. The architectural frame is bronze effect exactly like the effect given bronze metal work. I rather think it the handsomest and most agreeable piece of framing I ever saw. It is perfect in tone, and not too heavy though massive and architectural, and is fine against the shadowy dark background. The Madonna's face is sweet and deserves all the praise given it; all the other flesh painting, judged by modern standards, is very bad. St. Barbara's head has a sweet classic face. I like it only a little less than the Madonna. Without these two heads and by a nameless artist, I should not give it house room.

I was charmed with Rembrandt, Velasquez, Vandyke and Rubens. The school of Dutch painters, with their little ten by twelve inch panels, are wonderfully good and charming.

J. H. Moser

GEESE IN STREET — BOLKENHAIN

The trip from Dresden was uneventful except that I actually saw two storks standing on a big nest. They were on such a quaint ''lowly thatched cottage.'' I had read of storks when I was a little boy, and the tales Pa told of them fascinated me. Also saw a man re-roofing part of a house with thatch. He sat half-buried in straw, making little sheaves about six inches through, then laying them in courses like shingles, several deep. Hamburg is a vast commercial city with some curious old houses overhanging narrow canals, some interesting church spires and public buildings, and a very luxurious fashionable section. Two good-sized lakes in the very heart of the town with parklike surroundings, furnish it with a ''pair of lungs'' it could not well do without.

S.S. Perigrine, Hamburg. August 19.

My dear: I am leaving Germany, but it has been good to me, and I am grateful for treasures I have brought away, but home, my face turned in that direction, I am happier than I have been since I had the joy of reading your last letter.

J. H. Moser

LITTLE DUTCH BOY — HOLLAND — 1896

Letter to Alfred Zucker.
Paris. August 29.

I am in great luck to strike such weather, fine, exhilarating, a touch of autumn in it. Rained almost continually the past week in London. The Louvre I did thoroughly today from 9 till 2:30, no lunch or break. It overshadows Berlin, but Dresden has more good pictures, both numerically and in point of quality. I would not have missed the Louvre however, for now I can form a definite opinion of the value of the other collections I have seen.

No temple man is likely to build will ever be noble enough to form a worthy resting-place for the VENUS DE MILO! It is a divine work — all other art of every kind is tame, limited and human in comparison. Like ''Fuji'' in Japan — they except that always when speaking of their finest scenery, as though it were a deity and the rest only human. Oh, the Greeks! I have always had a reverence for the cast figures, but there is a subtle delicacy, a tenderness in the translucent, yellowed marble, that almost breathes — surely such are they that people the spheres.

I took a cab to the Luxemborg, only for a glance around. Here are the gems of living masters. That is the choicest collection of Moderns ever gathered under one roof, and justifies the French claim to be beyond all question ''the masters'' of the Moderns. This gallery is in wall space, probably not as large as the Academy of New York, but it is made up of ''holes in the wall,'' dozens of pictures any one of which would distinguish any collection of contemporary art. This is my gallery. I'd rather have that collection in my back yard then any I ever saw.

Jim.

81

J. H. Moser

VENUS DE MILO, PARIS — 1896

ILLUSTRATING FOR THE WASHINGTON TIMES

Moser docked in New York on September 18th and spent the fall in Cornwall until, at Al's insistence that he might be able to do some business in New York, he went down on December 4th. His initial efforts to make sales were not successful so, again urged by Alfred, he planned an exhibition at the new ''Bolkenhayn'' apartment on 5th Avenue for which he had painted a ceiling mural the previous winter. ''Never made so fine a show in excellence of pictures, place and light, or in such rich surroundings; but the rich people did not respond to invitations, and very few of my old friends turned out. Mr. Wycoff, whom I met on 'The Paris' going abroad, came down from Ithaca and bought one of my Bolkenhain studies, $200, which was my largest sale.'' James returned to Cornwall for Christmas and remained through the winter.

Early in July when he was again in New York, he got a letter from Stilson Hutchens, editor of the *Washington Times* asking him if he could do illustrations on a daily paper, ''quick, good, catchy, comical, sensible, etc.?'' Could you draw good heads like the enclosed on chalk plates and for transfer, etc.? Answer me quick, for I sail Tuesday on the 'Havel'.'' Moser's answer, ''I gladly accept your offer knowing I can do the work and feeling sure that we can agree on details. I got my start in Washington drawing for the New York dailies, the syndicates for Frank G. Carpenter and others.

Moser went down to Washington in September and stayed with the Blounts until he could find a home for his family. He soon found a pleasant small flat at 1220 G Street. It was ill furnished for occupancy, but drawing for the *''Times''* was arduous, often requiring night work so that he found the long trip to Georgetown and back time-consuming, and spent many nights in the flat.

To Martha. Home, 1220 G. Street. October 14, 1897.

My Dear: My Cesnors sketch and a big one of The Shoreham banquet to Bishop Keane, did the business. All at my feet tonight, and talking about the BIG NEW MAN they've got. I tell you it was an ovation. Mr. Hutchens is delighted to think I have won the office without his help, for they all opposed me; now they are all my fighting friends. . . . Mrs. Blount sent this check. I was astounded at it, her letter was beautiful. I'll copy it.

The Oaks, Georgetown. October 13, 1897.

Dear Jim: Some years ago you cast some bread upon the waters and I am under the impression that there are a few crumbs of that slice still due you — that is, if the Bible is true, and Providence doesn't forget to do his part. It has occurred to me that you ought to have your family here to keep you straight. Any man who stays out and goes on such a spree that he neither eats nor sleeps in his home for days, certainly needs looking after by someone who has the right to bring him to tow. In the interest of your moral character and of Mattie's happiness, I therefore enclose you a check on the American Security and Trust Company for $50. If my income were larger it would reach further, but I hope this amount will be sufficient to enable you to ''make the turn.'' There's luck in odd numbers and I hope that thirteen will prove a lucky number for you. With lots of love,

ever your friend, Lucia Eames Blount.

This bounty enabled Martha to bring the girls to Washington where they spent the first two weeks at the Blount's in Georgetown while James and Martha cleaned the flat and the long-stored furniture and settled in the little home.

The Ford - Batesville, Va
7 miles from Afton C.

H Moser - Oct 9 - 05

The Little Red Barn Studio - Cornwall.

83

HM.
Dec 7th 1906

HM - Jan 4
1910
"Pursie S.C."

SKETCHES by J. H. Moser

CLUBS OF ART STUDENTS
The Washington Times. December 10, 1899.
James Henry Moser

As the writer's pencil touches the paper to describe the young and flourishing Salmagundi Club of Washington, memory turns to that other Salmagundi Club in New York — the greatest of art clubs in this country, and the organization of all others most intimately associated with the inner lives of painter folk in America. Born in Sculptor Hartley's studio twenty-five years ago, and knowing the hardships of adversity, it has grown to be substantial and ideally comfortable. How well the writer, a member of the New York Salmagundi, remembers a never-to-be-forgotten winter night there three years ago, when Tyler, Dolph, Howe, Henry B. Smith, Green, Willing, Shelton, Shurtleff, Earl, Bacher, Baker, Volkmar, and many others gathered about the long table in the gallery after a joyous Bohemian dinner and, amid clouds of tobacco smoke, decorated the individual "steins" which now ornament the dado of the billiard room at the club house. There were weekly entertainments on "club nights," musicals, monotype parties; wonderful affairs; for these painters count among their intimate friends professional and amateur entertainers of the first rank. It may easily be imagined what notable evenings are spent at the Salmagundi Club during the New York season.

Like its famous namesake in New York, the Salmagundi Club here is a club made up of professional artists and students, most of them students at the Corcoran Art School. This club was organized to encourage more intimate social relations between the students, and to promote practical, effective work outside of school hours.

84

POE — THE ALLEN HOUSE — RICHMOND, VA. — 1883

J. H. Moser

85

J. H. Moser

THE OLD MILL — 1898

MOUNTAIN STREAM — INTERVALE, NEW HAMPSHIRE — 1895

J. H. Moser

J. H. Moser

THE OLD SMITHSONIAN BUILDING — 1895

WASHINGTON, D.C.

By the fall of 1898 Moser was writing periodic art columns for the *Times* in addition to his drawing, and by November was made instructor of a watercolor class at the Corcoran Gallery of Art. Though the salary was not large, this enabled him to give up drawing for the paper and was work that he enjoyed. He brought to it all his skill and enthusiasm so that in the ten years in which it was under his leadership, it came to be known as the most outstanding class of its kind in the country. In 1902, H. Siddons Mowbray, in a letter to Moser, said, "I was indeed very much impressed with your class work, and cannot recall in any other case such a high standard, and such excellent results."

During the winter Moser became secretary of the Society of Washington Artists. Already president of the Washington Water Color Club, a younger organization, he strove tirelessly to make all their exhibitions successful, and in every way possible worked for better art in the Capital. Meanwhile, his circle of friends and patrons in Washington and elsewhere were expanding, and he kept in close contact with the progress of art in New York and other large centers, for he felt and often said, that an artist could not do his best work unless he kept in touch by seeing current exhibitions.

Each year when the schools closed in June, Martha and the girls went to the old homestead in Cornwall, Connecticut. James usually joined them for a while though he felt that most of his summer should be spent at resorts in the Adirondacks, White Mountains, Berkshires, or in the Blue Mountains of the south, where he could sell his work as well as produce pictures representative of different parts of the country.

In 1901 Moser was invited to send two pictures to the Pan American Exposition in Buffalo. He stayed in Washington until the middle of July, then went up to Buffalo and on to Toronto, Canada, for a short visit with his mother's family.

Riverside Inn, Saranac Lake. July 29.

To Martha: "I have seen the Art Gallery. The building is not as large as the New York Academy, but it is crammed full of gems. Just as I expected, this is a rare opportunity to study the best Americans — and as there are only the best, one does not have to hunt for pictures to study."

Back in God's country once more and I am not a bit sorry. Canada is all right, but I don't feel at home in a country where the streets are full of vermillion — red-coated soldiers and Union Jack — a strange money — I had no idea Canada would seem so foreign, England is not more so.

Ride over the mountains by Chateaugay railroad the view was immense — sunshine and rain. From the top of the grade near Chazy Lake I could see Lake Champlain with its islands, and the Green Mountains beyond. To the west, Adirondacks, with the valley dotted with lakes — pictures everywhere. Arriving in the rain, the darkey porter with whom I got on good terms though not one of his passengers, told me of this hotel. New House, clean and neat. I got a cheap room, dormer under the roof. Just by luck, I think it is the finest room for mountain observation and study I ever had. It is a great thing to get a room that looks out on fine scenery for one gets a chance to catch fleeting effects that are so valuable.

89

J. H. Moser

BLUE ADIRONDACKS MOUNTAINS — 1902

THE CORCORAN SCHOOL OF ART

The watercolor class has grown so large and important that it has become desirable to place its management in abler professional hands. Mr. Moser is widely known for his skill and versatility in this medium. His work is as well and favorably known in New York as it is here. He is a member of the American Water Color Club and Secretary of the Society of Washington Artists — an enthusiastic worker and an optimist. Mr. Moser will popularize this class and do much toward increasing local interest in this delightful art.

Hints to Students

Do not try to paint before you can draw correctly and easily with charcoal. . . . Train your hand and eye to work from memory. Much freedom and facility come from this practice. Fill book after book . . . you will find the practice of immense value in your more serious work. And when the book is full, tear out the few good sketches which are worth preserving, and destroy the rest. Keep the book clean. Do not get into the slovenly habit of drawing on both sides of the page, for pencil sketches smear so dreadfully.

Landscape Painting

The custom now, . . . is to paint pictures directly from nature and often at a single sitting, but this is not the way some of the best works have been produced. Every painter to succeed must go constantly to nature and must learn from her, but it is not necessary that he copy nature exactly, his privilege being to complete her intention. It is not always possible to paint a picture on the instant that one sees an inspiring subject, but if one goes armed with a sketch book even the most fleeting effects can be captured and preserved for future use.

Working from Sketches and Notes

With the utmost simplicity and directness the artist jots down outstanding facts, first in lines then in words. The chief features of the view will be indicated and around the margin of the sketch will be such notations as ''water lower in tone than sky, outline of mountain almost lost against dark cloud.'' Sometimes in the margin will be tiny notes of color, or just a little scale of tones, not a great deal, but fully enough to prevent untruth in interpretation.

Sketches

Unless a student can directly draw a cup and saucer on a table he should not attempt or expect to be able to draw a tree by the roadside. A sketch is not a careless drawing, a few lines of colors jotted down indiscriminately, but rather a thoughtful study of structures and values, avoiding superfluous detail. Picture what you see and not what you think you ought to see.

Corcoran Students Exhibition

At the end of the school year, in May, the school held an annual exhibition of the students' work. One year some of the instructors allowed their students to make the selections and arrangements to suit themselves, but Moser, in his concern for excellence, was more strict with his class. The Hemicycle Hall was turned over to the instructor of watercolor for his class exhibit. Out of 250 drawings submitted he selected 107, the work of twenty-nine pupils which quite filled the handsome, well lighted gallery.

J. H. Moser

"BOWL OF ROSES"
Painted in Class, 1908 — Corcoran School of Art, Washington, D.C.

The pupils had nothing whatever to do with the selection and arrangement, and though the instructor regretted sincerely the absence of pictures by some members in this exhibition of the year's work, he could not deviate from the rules set down when he assumed control of the class. With that control went responsibilities which he felt keenly, and the present exhibition of watercolors stands for his conception of what a class exhibition should be, namely, uniform in mounting and arrangement, no drawing to be shown which does not deserve a good place, and a good light, and above all, no drawing to be shown upon which the instructor's brush has been placed.

Art Notes

When an exhibition comes along do not shove forward some prize picture or study done years ago. Stand or fall by the work you are doing now, and above all, don't talk of medals, honors and successes you have won. That is the province of the dealer, against which there can be no sensible objection, and you can trust him to work it for all he is worth.

Art Topics

People buy what they want if the price suits them. It is folly to tell them what they ought to have. The dealer's existence depends largely on that course; the painter's does not. His is a dual life, devoted unselfishly to higher art as only a few understand it. He lives frugally, takes contracts to get a living, and paints every last brilliant button on the uniform, or every picket in the fence about the farmhouse, if the patron demands it, but his ambition does not stop there. He strives in every hour that can be spared from his "business" to be true to his ideals. Some day he is discovered and a market is suddenly created for the best, and only the best, he can do. That is fame, but he will never be happier than in the dear days of his striving.

Moser's Method of Painting

Before he put the brush to paper, Moser had his plan firmly in mind and the method he planned to follow. For this reason he welcomed watchers while he was working, and often entertained them by the hour with anecdotes and stories while working freely and fast all the time.

It might not be out of place to mention here his method of painting misty mountain pictures for which he came to be particularly well known. He started by wetting the paper. Using a large, soft brush, he washed down across the paper in wide horizontal swaths adding sky tints as he desired, then lining in distant mountains with a pale blue and as he advanced, adding more pigment to the blue line of nearer mountains, and finally foreground shades. While the paper was still wet, at just the right moment, he blotted out with bits of soft blotting paper, patches and spots for cloud effects. Some detail was added while the paper was still wet, but the final finishing was usually done when the paper was completely dry.

He's got a good size Salon of his own
He can paint a dandy picture in a rush
And we can certify the skill he's shown
In using of most any kind of brush
When he's hoppin' in and out among his paints
With his palette and his canvass, never fear
A happy day with Jimmie, on the rush
Will last a connoisseur for a year

So heres to yer Jimmie Moser
You do more than many can
You're a bully story teller
And a firstclass painting man
We gives you a certificate
And if you want it signed,
Every one of us will do it
Whenever you're inclined

TRIBUTE TO JAMES HENRY MOSER FROM HIS WATERCOLOR CLASS CORCORAN SCHOOL OF ART

Perhaps some of the reasons for the success of Moser's class may be found in these excerpts from one of his own art columns in the "*Post*" a few years later. May, 1902. "The art teacher whose ambition is that his pupils shall early learn the great truths that have come to him by a process sadly effortful and slow, finds an enjoyment in class work that is scarcely equalled by the welcome and applause that greets some successful new product of his own mind and brush."

Then there is the sharpening of one's critical faculty and a widening of one's horizon, that are as exhilarating as mountain air. It is an indescribable pleasure to do something new and original oneself, but the pleasure of seeing young minds who follow one's lead with unwavering faith for a couple of seasons, make pictures revealing qualities some painters have not reached in a lifetime of effort, is a pleasure deep and lasting. It is a confirmation of one's faith that the secret beauty of things lies very near the surface when the cobwebs of ignorance and old, worn-out theories have once been brushed away and the eyes see not what seems to be the truth, but what really is the truth.

93

THE NEW CENTURY

On January first it was the writer's pleasure to stand at the foot of the Memorial Cross on University Heights, and there see the Capitol and the Monument and the beautiful city in the bright, crisp sunlight of the first morning of the first year of the new century.

It was a dream of beauty. The city was wrapped in an opalescent haze, through which snow-covered roofs glistened like burnished silver. The Capitol, the Library, and the Monument rose solemn and stately on either side like the handles of a loving cup — a vision to make one proud of his native land and of his home city. The morning was bitterly cold and the wind piercing. The benumbed fingers could scarce hold the pencil so anxious to record in hurried shorthand the lines and color scheme of this glorious scene. It was a vision of brightness, one of those glimpses of the possibilities of nature on which poets build their pictures of the celestial city. There was in this picture with the winter sunshine streaming toward the beholder, something of the joy and gladness one associates with Easter.

This impression was emphasized perhaps, by the memory of the sunset low and rich, shadowy and mysterious, and not without a touch of sadness in it, which the writer had witnessed from Bennings Bridge the night before. A sunset passing from colorful brilliance where the sun, a flaming ball of molten gold in a field of crimson, dropped behind the sharp contour of the Capitol dome — to the pale green afterglow, when lights began to flicker about the powerhouse and the Library.

From beginning to end it inspired memories of the pictures unpainted, the good resolutions broken, and all those thoughts which come to him who, from some fine point of view on New Year's Eve watches until driven homeward by the cold and the dark.

But the glorious morning effect, when the sun was well up and the scene flooded with sunshine, was one portending mighty and splendid things. The most dismal and confirmed pessimist standing there at that moment, must have renewed his acquaintance with hope.

The Washington Times. January 7, 1900.
James Henry Moser.

J. H. Moser

95

WASHINGTON WINTER LANDSCAPE WITH CAPITOL

J. H. Moser

THE APPLE SEED SKETCH

A little girl observing her father's carelessness in forming the written letter "*a*," remarked: "Papa, that is not right; teacher says you must first draw an apple, so, '*o*', and then put a tail to it, to '*a*'." Now, it was not an egg, nor yet a bean, nor any other of the many oval forms in nature with which all children are familiar — it was an apple seed, with its nicely-graduated oval till it reaches the upper end, where it comes sharply to a point, making exactly the shape of the body of a nicely-formed "*a*."

In the apple seed sketch, out of which the "*a*" was made, lies the text of an art talk. That child who is taught to observe nature closely, and note its peculiarities, and who goes through life with eye alert and hand trained to hold the pencil, grows up possessed of the key to more pure, wholesome enjoyment than ever comes to the un-trained eye.

In the present watercolor exhibition of local paint-ers it is entertaining to watch the effect of the different pictures on the throng of visitors who chat before the watercolors in the pretty gallery. Some of them, who profited in childhood by the "apple seed sketch," and were led from this little experience to observe nature, go from picture to picture, making intelligent comments and getting the keenest enjoyment out of this array of modest bits of white paper, upon which the colors have been spread with such magic. Here are fleeting effects of light and atmosphere — the subtle color melody of a rose, and the tender harmony of flesh tints and sparkling eyes, all given like life, and, something more, for that indefinable quality which marks the artist's personality is also here.

Methods of Painting in Watercolor

There are four distinct schools. The first is the early method in which the English excel. A pure transparent wash of color spread over the entire paper — this being repeated after drying the paper until these successive layers produce the desired effect. Detail and strength is imparted by repeated washes of transparent color in parts of the picture.

The second method is rather French and Italian. In this, after the drawing is made in pencil, patches of color are placed where they belong of the exact color and strength desired at that point, and they are often never touched again. When a dark patch and a light one are side by side, and both are still wet, a fine line of the paper is allowed to remain between them. This prevents the two patches or tints running into each other and gives a very fascinating sparkle to the finished picture. By some this is considered the true province of watercolor. It is a delightful method, especially adapted to rapid sketching from nature.

That method by which the most distinguished and altogether satisfactory results are obtained is a combina-tion of these methods with the addition of Chinese white, which is a thick opaque white and imparts qualities that are distinctly like oil painting in appearance. This is called the Dutch school. The possibilities of watercolor in this method are almost limitless, for it combines the fine qualities of the transparent method and also is able to produce qualities that have been thought to belong exclusively to oil and pastel.

The fourth method, is the entirely opaque where the colors, resembling the tube oil paints, are used solidly precisely as a painter in oil places his colors on the canvas. The finished picture in this method resembles oil except that it does not have the shine of an oil painting.

APPLE BLOSSOMS

J. H. Moser

THE COLOR GREEN

One of the most frequent questions asked by students just beginning to paint out of doors is "How shall I paint green trees?" Every painter of experience knows that green is the simplest part of the problem. Any field of flat green is a crude statement of the fact. I remember well when as a boy in school how the map of South America when, tinted green, as we frequently painted it "just for fun," would resemble a tree, and, being more interested in trees than I ever was in geography, South America still looks like a tree to me. On sketching tours I sometimes come upon a tree possessing that shape and then my mind reverts to those drowsy summer days when it seemed as though 4 o'clock would never come.

So much for green. Trees are green, and the outline sketched correctly the little field it makes may be filled with any green, the darker the better, and you have a fair, if only a bald, statement of a tree. One should be sure to hold this simple statement intact in any other efforts to be truer and more refined in the representation.

Once sure of this green note in trees and landscapes one must strive to find those subtle greys which modify the greens and bring out all those delicate relations which develop the relative value of the different objects in the picture and the aerial prospective. This is a process which requires close observation and a discriminating taste — for it is not necessary to concern one's self with everything in the picture to know just what objects and what details are the ones most deserving of attention. This is what one learns by studying pictures — close, thoughtful study of nature, and many failures.

Twachtman, the great New York landscape painter and teacher, speaking of the danger of seeing greens too pure, says: "When you paint green try not so much to match the green of the grass as to consider it in its relation to the sky and other parts. Mr. Wier once said when painting that as he finished his sketch he suddenly discovered his picture was the only green thing to be seen."

There-in is the whole secret. The look of the woods was doubtless at first sight very green, but green paint which was perhaps a good match for any weed Mr. Wier might have plucked from the mass at his feet was not a match for it the moment that same weed was some distance from him and a part of the landscape he was painting. When green trees and grass pass beyond the immediate foreground they partake of reflections from the sky and innumerable other sources, and the atmosphere has its effect, so that green pure and simple as it comes in the watercolor box or the oil tube is no longer a match for it. Then it is that the shadows partake of blues, greys, and at times purple, and the lights are silvered and violet — not so pronounced, perhaps, as some of the impressionists would have us believe, but still here, with great distinctness for those who have eyes to see. For instance, Corot's pictures are invariably landscapes representing spring or summer, and yet how rarely does one come away from a Corot with an impression of green lingering in the memory. No; green was not the beauty of the scene as Corot saw it. To him there were certain silvery harmonies or black masses of shadowy trees, tender and full of poetry, and it was these beauties which the great master of landscape painted with such intelligence and delight.

The Washington Times. July 1, 1900.
James Henry Moser.

98

J. H. Moser

WHITE BIRCHES — 1892

THE HILLS OF CORNWALL

As I write these lines in my old summer studio in "The Hills of Cornwall," far up by Litchfield in the extreme northwestern corner of Connecticut, my thoughts revert to those other days, when I roamed about here, year in and year out, painting the lake, the hills, the brooks and beautiful villages. Those were the palmy days when pictures sold themselves, a blessing the true artist can understand. What a delight it was, that bright day when I knocked out the north wall of the big loft over the carriage house and put in a studio window there, set up my easel, and launched out as a landscape painter in the midst, not of his patrons, but of his material. No genial dealer said to me, "Paint a dozen of this," and no good-natured, but misguided patron said, "Change this," or "that," "I don't know anything about art, but I know what I like."

Nature with infinite sympathy and most appealing look pointed to the masters saying, "Remember them and follow me." What a joy it was! And when the spring came and the portfolios were full to bursting with the year's work, good Mr. Fischer would throw open his doors and invite his friends to see the Cornwall pictures. Then my cup of happiness was full. So it came about that the Cornwall hills are familiar to Washington.

Cornwall, in Litchfield County, Connecticut, lies in the foothills on the western border range of the vale of Berkshire. Here the valley ceases to be, and the clear waters of the rippling Housatonic pass through a narrow gap in the mountain. West Cornwall and Cornwall Bridge are the railroad stations. By train, Cornwall seems a wilderness of rocky mountainside covered with birch and scrub pine. The wonder to the stranger ever is that these pretty little villages mentioned should exist in this wild and isolated place, where there is scarcely a single city block of approximately level ground. There are good, much-used roads in sight, but the way out and the reason for their being is not clear. It is only when one leaves the river and reaches the interior some one hundred feet above it that the lovely, rolling upland meadows and beautiful farm homesteads appear. Then one discovers a fertile country intersected by broad stone walls that tell of endless and patient toil in clearing these rock strewn "Hills of Cornwall."

Here overlooking the beautiful Cream Hill Lake is the old farm, where for generations back the parents of my children have lived, loved, toiled and served God in that good old New England fashion which made a type of American men and women which are the admiration of the world. I never cease to wonder at the tidiness and esthetic taste with which these New England people keep up all of their utilitarian surroundings. Possessing artistic taste though they never dream of such a thing they are apt to call it neatness and look upon it simply as a sign of thrift.

Cream Hill, 1900 feet above sea level and 900 feet above the railroad at West Cornwall is a huge hemisphere containing four or five square miles of highly cultivated ground. It is the garden spot of Cornwall yet quite as much a mountain as those great forest-covered ones surrounding it. There is a background of wooded hills surrounding the plains and farmhouses, and barns set in picture meadows. Brooks and a pine forest scarcely excelled in beauty and grandeur by the Cathedral Woods at Intervale, and Cream Hill Lake, three miles away, call forth universal praise. They are a pride of Cornwall.

Washington Times. August 19, 1900.

SCOVILLE FARM — 1908

J. H. Moser

AUTUMN COLOR PAINTING

This year the Housatonic River Valley was exceptionally brilliant. The frosts were very late and not until October 19, when there was a freeze that covered the shallow ponds with ice, did the oak trees, the last to change their rugged green leaves to crimson with the frost's bidding, join the yellow birches, maples and chestnuts in a superb pageant of color. The mountainside changes almost in a night from green to the splendor of burnished gold. This wealth of rich tints was backed up by a clear blue sky of June's intensity. The magnificence of such a color display may not be adequately described. Orange-yellow is the prevailing tone, but it is a mosaic of every possible shade of yellow and red with russets and leathery tones of exquisite beauty. It is this marvelous mixing of bright and somber color with the tender feeling of atmosphere which makes so gorgeous an arrangement harmonious — it is never crude or jarring on one's color sense.

The season of bright colors is so short, it is exasperating to a painter. Today he plants his easel before a maple whose burden of cadmium orange makes the long looked for note in a picture he has planned. He lays in the masses of color and gets a fine start. Finally, at the day's close, chilled and uncomfortable, he packs his outfit and trudges back to the hotel, happy in the thought that he will return tomorrow and complete his study. Tomorrow comes with leaden skies, the wind is in the east, and by 9 o'clock it has settled to a steady rain, which continues till 4 o'clock in the afternoon. When it ceases to pour the clouds lift on the western horizon and a pale lemon-yellow streak of sky appears, which later turns to a delicate apple green, with flakes of brilliant salmon and orange floating upon it. Of course, the painter has seen all this, for when the rain ceased he left the work he had been happily engaged upon all day — a picture, a mountain memory which he elaborated from the pencil sketch, some beautiful fleeting effect he had observed on some previous tramp over the hills.

The painter has no dull, cheerless, rainy days. Those are the valued opportunities to work up his memory notes. When the rain stops he slips into his rubber boots and, with a sketch book in hand, starts out for sunset notes. He knows well that for richness and tone no sunsets equal those which follow an autumnal rainy day. When the morrow arrives, clear and bright, he starts out to finish his "maple tree study," and, arriving at the spot, he can scarcely believe his senses. A naked tree with only here and there a pale yellow leaf clinging to the sighing branches; all that remains of the splendid garment the tree so proudly wore less than two days before. Artists soon get used to such disappointments, though, happily, nature seldom produces such changes as this. If he is inexperienced he will sit down there and try to finish his study, but if he is wise he will go back to his room at the hotel — his improvised studio — and finish it there, and at once, relying on his recollection, making the most of a fresh memory, for delays are dangerous.

It is surprising how rapidly impressions fade. They may not entirely disappear, but they so soon mingle with other impressions that, from a pencil sketch a week old, it may be difficult to get anything like a true picture. These should always be worked up in color at the earliest possible moment.

The Washington Times. October 28, 1900.

102

103

POND HILL IN OCTOBER — 1905

J. H. Moser

REFLECTIONS OF A COUNTRY ARTIST

It was the beginning of a "January Thaw." From zero weather the thermometer rose to forty degrees, remaining there all night long. The morning was mild and vapory. Water dripped from the eaves. Fences and bar-posts looked bare and gaunt without their familiar hoods of snow. The distant hills were very blue — dark wood-lots, the quality and color of slate, cut strange figures in the patchwork of whitened fields. Cold emerald green places began to appear in the rye-lot, and over them — those restless, glittering bits of jet black — the crows, gathered to scold the soft air.

The roads became umber streaks across the snow. Puddles of yellow water wore miniature rivers to the road's edge, there pouring a little ocherish flood into the ditches. Big drifts, that once covered the stone walls shrank respectfully away upon the approach of the south-wind. Gray lichens and green moss, equally quick to feel the return of comparative warmth, began to grow, imparting a juicy richness to the color of rocks and old decrepit fence-rails. Briar patches, grown up about the boulders in the "half moon meadow," made beautiful foreground studies, finely relieved by wide mat-like margins of snow.

The fog drifted up and down in clouds over the hills throughout the morning. The effects suggested unfinished pictures — great masses rubbed in, as when an artist is feeling his way upon a new canvas — here and there a bit of detail perfectly developed.

The afternoon is balmy and springlike. I decide upon a tramp across the lake.

Stepping from slippers into rubber boots and having felt in my pocket to be sure that sketch book and pencils are there, I start off. My way leads under the yellow tipped willows where, at the roadside spring — a red rusted half barrel makes a sort of tub, into which, from a mossy black wooden trough, pours the clear spring water. With its surrounding moss-covered rocks, the spring makes a spot of rich dark color in the snow. The ice is a foot thick upon the lake. Under the snow on the surface of the ice is an inch of water. Through this I plod, leaving tracks upon the white field black as my rubber boots.

Continuing my walk across the lake, I come upon tangles of dark green, metallic leaved laurel filling the deeper places in the woods — an inviting carpet of wintergreen, red stemmed and with leaves all shades of crimson, purple, bronze and dark green. Beneath the stiff, leathery leaves, that glisten so brightly, clustering berries are striving to hide scarlet blushes.

The gray that overspread my afternoon has given place to a clear color-full sunlight that has a hint of evening which turns me homeward. Once more upon the broad white surface of the lake I find the purple-gray of the surrounding hills has deepened to a more solemn note.

The sunset is one of indescribable splendor. Its wealth of color soon dies away, leaving a sky of pale lavender and green, deepening to rose. The new moon and a single bright star appear. Below this field of soft poetic light is spread a dark landscape of great depth and mystery — and the snow.

105

WOODS IN EARLY SPRING

J. H. Moser

J. H. Moser

CHESAPEAKE & OHIO CANAL, GEORGETOWN, D.C.

Night scene on the C&O Canal attracted a great deal of attention at the exhibition of the Boston Art Club as well as in subsequent exhibitions.

The Boston transcript wrote of its delightful novel tone, simplicity of design and coloring. Moser refused an offer to purchase it by William T. Evans.

Exhibited:
American Water Color
    Society, New York, 1902
Universal Exposition,
    St. Louis, 1904
Morrey Gallery, Washington,
    D.C., 1905
Lewis & Clark Centennial
    Exposition, Portland,
    Oregon, 1905

GREEN BRIDGE LIGHT

J. H. Moser

SKETCHING AT KEENE VALLEY
The Tahawus House, Keene Valley.
September 11, 1901.

My Dear: I arrived this evening from Upper Ausable Lake where Shurtleff, Frank McCombs and I spent the night sleeping on a bed of balsam boughs in a log hut facing a huge fire on the shore of the lake, six miles from a wagon road or even a trail that a man could follow on horseback. Only a man with a pack basket could follow that mile "carry" from the lower lake to the upper one, where our guide had another boat and brought us to this camp of his. This is famous as the finest place in the mountains. Rainbow Cascade beggars description! I was not surprised when Shurtleff said Wyant sat there and worked six weeks on studies, then went home and worked all winter on a picture then painted it out! Inness sat there. James Bristol, William Hart, Fitch and others sketched about here.

Shurtleff's Cottage, Keene Valley.
October 11, 1901.

Shurtleff and I worked out in the woods morning and afternoon — it was delightful and I got some good sketches. They treat me in such a sweet home-folksey way, I enjoy it and am sorry I cannot be with them longer. I asked Shurtleff if he ever painted on Sunday. "Never a brush stroke," said he, "though I have been sorely tempted." "I believe a man who works all the week at one thing should have an entire rest and change one day in the seven." He is such an interesting man, and repeats over and over, "You don't know how much good it has done me to have you up here, Moser." He is doing some fine things, but he weaves his pictures in a mysterious way, painting in and out, out and in, and feeling his way with broad slashes till after a while when he strikes it, he strikes it hard.

Washington Star. December 6, 1902.

Mr. Moser has been winning laurels for himself and our local art, his watercolor entitled "Boat Carnival" in the New York Watercolor Club's annual, and the canvas picturing a bit of Cornwall Lake which is in the Copley exhibition in Boston, being generally mentioned by discriminating critics as among the most notable paintings in the respective shows. When it is remembered that such men as Sargent, La Farge, Snell, Winslow Homer and Easton, are contributors to these exhibitions, and that mere admission is adjudged as honor; the full significance of this compliment becomes plain.

Richmond Despatch. May 17, 1903.

Mr. J. H. Moser, known as widely for his fine work as Art Critic of the *Washington Post* as from the fact that he is ex-president of the Washington Water Color Club, the winner of the first Corcoran prize for watercolor, a medalist of the Atlanta and Charleston expositions, an instructor in watercolor at the Corcoran Art School, and a painter whose individuality of tone and treatment have won him a distinctive rank among the artists of the day, is already a Richmond favorite; one of his watercolors, "Sunrise at Virginia Beach" having been especially admired at the exhibition of the Art Club last year.

Visitors to the annual New York, Washington, and Baltimore exhibitions and to the Corcoran Gallery, are familiar with Mr. Moser's style as a watercolorist. He will have a number of picture at the exhibit in this city opening tomorrow. One of the best of these is catalogued as "Morning on the Upper James." All are characterized by the freshness and delicacy of touch which give great charm to whatever comes from Mr. Moser's brush.

109

SUNRISE — VIRGINIA BEACH

J. H. Moser

Joseph Jefferson.
Washington Post. November 24, 1901.
James Henry Moser

On opening my studio door recently in answer to the clang of the clumsy old iron sphynx knocker on the door, I had the happiness to welcome the beloved Mr. Jefferson — actor painter — to my studio. He had come in response to an invitation to see the unfinished Adirondack picture I was making for the annual exhibition of the American Watercolor Society in April.

Mr. Jefferson and I indulged in a heart to heart talk over the work of those Dutch Masters whom we both adore. Just at this time he was rejuvenated, bubbling over with joy in the possession of a new "Keever" he had just purchased from Mr. Fischer; and I fancied when I saw with what evident pleasure he put expression and charm into his "Caleb Plummer" that evening at the National, he was thinking of his new art treasure.

I was greatly amused by Mr. Jefferson's praise of a picture on my studio wall — a deep-toned landscape with a brook and footbridge in the foreground. Finally he said with suspicion: "That is like my subjects." "No, no," I protested. Putting on his glasses, he examined it closely, and finding his distinguished autograph in the corner he exclaimed, "It is mine; that's the picture I sent you. That is a good joke. I didn't think I could paint as well as that." I assured him his painting was better than he realized and that this picture he sent me a year ago is one of his best.

Mr. Jefferson, with all his profound knowledge and love of art, is not without that ever-present humor which endears him to all who know him.

Speaking of monotypes and methods, he explained how he painted with a pallette knife, feathers, sponges, rags, anything; in fact very little with brushes. Picking up a rag, he showed me how deftly he managed it. Effect, tone, color, are what he seeks; not details on which the eye lights without seeing the whole picture which we all know must be accomplished first at any cost.

Monotypes in color are his latest experiment, and in telling how the blurred impression is so much more artistic than the painted picture on copper from which the single impression is taken, he told an amusing incident which occurred once when he was playing in Edinburgh. A noted lady visitor who happened in while he was painting, sat down on a freshly painted oil sketch which had occupied the chair first. Her distress may be imagined, and it is worth a good deal to hear Mr. Jefferson tell the story. "Oh, Mr. Jefferson," she said, "whatever shall I do? I have ruined your beautiful painting." "Not a bit of it," he hastened to reply, and holding the sketch up for her to see, all of those present were agreed that the added mystery of blended colors and softened line had really improved the picture.

NOTE: Joseph Jefferson was an American actor born in Philadelphia in 1829 and died in 1905. He was well known for appearances in New York as "Dr. Pangloss" and "Our American Cousin." He became world famous for his part as "Rip Van Winkle," first produced at the Adelphi Theatre in London, 1865.

111

Joseph Jefferson

OLD MAN CROSSING MOUNTAIN STREAM
PRESENTED TO J. H. MOSER BY JOSEPH JEFFERSON

THE TYPHOID EPIDEMIC

In 1904 Washington was in the throes of a typhoid fever epidemic, but regardless of this James spent the whole summer in the City, while his family was in Connecticut, because his father who was living in Atlanta, Georgia with his daughter Eda, was seriously ill. He died in September.

James's family returned the latter part of September and early in October his older daughter, Grace, in spite of all precautions, came down with the dread disease. A week later Lydia was taken to the hospital with the fever, followed shortly by her mother.

When Martha was taken to the hospital, he wired Cornwall and asked his wife's sister, Lydia Scoville, to come down. She came and kept house until after Christmas when all were recovered; then she took Grace back with her. What James went through during those terrible months of illness can best be understood from a letter he wrote to his old friend Lydia Hubbard, which follows:

January 22, 1905.

My dear Lydia: Your welcome letter of New Years greeting found me just emerging from my first real trial in life. Fate has waited too long, a man's life at fifty can't be spoiled, he's had it! And mine is a record I challenge anyone to surpass, for health and continued happiness; so when the jolt came, I went on just the same looking after details and selling pictures. They had every care, doctors, nurses and hospital. Father's illness all summer, and death early in September left me to begin the winter all but "broke."

You can imagine how hard hit I was. Lydia developed pneumonia with typhoid; Grace and Mattie had it simply. For three weeks I was given plainly to understand that Lydia could not recover. I frankly gave up on her, concentrating my thoughts on saving the others who were, for a spell, in critical condition. I threw aside entirely the dread fact that I was logically the next victim, and took particular care of my health. I gave instructions that no messages were to be sent me from the hospital after dark, and slept soundly. I knew they never needed a well dad with his head on his shoulders so much as then. Lill came down and ran the house just as Mattie would have done — she was my tower of strength.

As I look back my grim attitude seems amusing, but now that they are well, I feel like an old man, sore and weary-headed as if I'd gone through some prolonged mental and physical battle. I had good luck, sold $500 worth of watercolors in a few weeks, some to people who did not know my family was ill, so I was able to carry the burden alone. I brought Mama home Thanksgiving Day. Lydia was unconscious for so long and such a skeleton. Even when I brought her home after Christmas, with her head shaved, she was still mostly knees, ribs and feet, but one can see her grow like a baby, from day to day.

Grace and Lill will probably go to Cornwall next week; Mattie and Lydia early in spring, so you see "the fire is out and the engines have gone home." I have not accomplished much in painting in the last few months. My watercolor class at the Corcoran is getting on fine; I enjoy the work so much, and am still doing my weekly column for the *Post*.

113

WASH DAY — MAY, 1897

J. H. Moser

NOTES OF ART AND ARTISTS
Washington Post. April 2, 1905.
James Henry Moser

John W. Alexander is the only American painter whose electric technique of the Velasquez-Hals type, may be said to command the attention and share world honors with Sargent and Zorn. Mr. Alexander's method is quite as individual and personal, if not more so, than either of his brilliant rivals in this particular field. This artist also reveals at times a depth of sentiment in his work; a mighty consideration in great figure painting, which the other two painters seem entirely insensitive to. . . . Close examination of the canvas here, discloses a simplicity of technique and purity of color that must be lasting and a stumbling block to all groping craftsmen. Mr. Alexander is painting a bit solider and is more colorful than formerly and his pictures are stronger for it.

It is always interesting to hear a master on his own point of view and aims. It therefore seems timely to offer a letter from him on the subject just now when the reader may study so good an example as the one here, and with the painter's explanation, learn exactly what he is endeavoring to accomplish. The letter was received two years ago when ''The Ray of Sunlight,'' that great painting and musical expression, was awarded the first Corcoran Gallery prize. This picture, by the way, was recently purchased for a western museum.

Mr. Alexander wrote: I was so pleased by your article in *''The Post''* on my ''Ray of Sunlight'' that I wrote to Mrs. Barney for your address.

So much nonsense has been written on my method of painting that it was a real delight to come across a sane article like yours, and it has given me courage to write to you in the same way.

The purest white mixed with the purest turpentine is very soon the color of tallow. I have now for at least fifteen years used nothing but benzine which evaporates almost immediately leaving the color as pure as it can be. I have gone one point further and have all my canvases made without oil in the ground, and as porous as possible to admit of drying, and I'll tell you exactly what that method is. In the first place you evidently believe that I am serious in my work, and that I would not adopt a method that would not give the best possible results.

I have been experimenting for more years than I care to admit, and it was an easy thing to prove that oil and varnish would soon darken, but I found also that turpentine would do the same thing. I have had no oil, varnish, or turpentine in my studio for years. Another point; my pictures are not so thin as they look. The actual weight in color would surprise you, but the effect of thinness is given by the heavy grain of the canvas, and by the technique, which consists mainly in rubbing the color well into the canvas. As you say, this does not affect the durability of a picture. Some of the most brilliant works of the old masters are hardly more than a wash. It is the heavily painted picture that cracks.

Thanking you for your article, and feeling sure you will understand the spirit of this letter, I am

Very truly yours,
John W. Alexander.

114

115

FIREWORKS ACROSS THE POTOMAC — 1902   *(Oil — 19 x 29)*

J. H. Moser

WEDDING ANNIVERSARY
To Martha. October 18, 1906.

Best of all:

You will observe that the date is quite plainly indicated in this eventful epistle. You will not need glasses to read it! I never took much stock in the date as you well know. It was an anxious, headachey day with a mob around, when I was dying to have you alone somewhere, where we could talk and I could just kiss you and kiss you and kiss you forever.

It took some years for me to realize what a prize I had won — and what times we had had, Matt dear. Some bumps and jolts, but we have never doubted that God made us for each other. . . . Age creeps on apace and we cannot but feel some anxiety for our material welfare, but our hearts are still young and our courage strong, and our love secure and mutual. Worry doesn't help, and we have ceased to hope for many things we once believed our happiness depended on. The little we shall need I am sure we shall find through a kindly Providence, so long as our health holds out; and when that goes, we shall be near the end, and it will not matter much. We will have had very full and happy lives and we will, I feel sure, find ways and means to keep ourselves from being a burden on anyone. So on this ''hundredth anniversary'' of our wedding day, I am happier and more content and hopeful than on any day since the ever blessed event. . . . I'm thrilled through to think how soon I shall be home again.

Hugs and kisses for the girlies and a double share for ''Her best of All.''

Thine and theirs till the ''Crack o' Doom''
Jim.

By 1906 Moser's reputation was well established. There was no other artist so completely identified with the art life of the Capitol as he, while at the same time he held a wide interest in the larger art centers, and was always ready to lend a hand in smaller, struggling art communities: Richmond, Knoxville, Atlanta, St. Louis, Cincinnati. His work was welcomed in all the prominent exhibitions and his pictures were praised and selected for reproduction in the press, while quotations from his weekly art column in the *Washington Post* were frequent.

His versatility in reproducing all aspects of nature was unquestioned, but he gloried in days whose colors were softened by cloud or mist, and in cloud effects. Some of his most powerful dramatizations were of clouds hanging heavy over great mountain peaks, or partially obscuring the valleys in between.

After the watercolor exhibition the *Washington Herald* makes this comment on the Moser pictures. ''There are six in all and the two large studies are finished examples of the particular line of work in which Mr. Moser surpasses most other landscape painters. It was once said of him, 'Moser knows how to paint the air'. If this is not the technical truth, it is close to it. In 'Morning on the Allegheny River', Mr. Moser has struck a note of preeminence. It may be mist or fog, or cloud miasma — and through it a delicate mauve and gray opens to the sky. The effect is incomparably beautiful, full of action and atmospheric transference. Equally delicate in treatment, though hardly as emotional in effect, is 'Whiteface Mountain on Lake Placid'. It is Whiteface at the quiet hour of sunset, surrounded by caressing clouds, and faintly crimsoned at its highest point.''

HMOSER-

CLOUDS OVER THE MOUNTAIN

J. H. Moser

DAUGHTER GRACE'S WEDDING
From Martha Moser to Her Mother
December 29, 1907.

Grace's Jim came Thursday A.M. December 19; after a little visit here he went down to the Forest Service office and found Mr. Pinchot and arrangements were settled right off that he should stay here for three months, so he came back very happy. He says he doesn't see any reason why he shouldn't take Grace back with him. He doesn't want to go without her, thinks a year out west would be pleasant for her and she can go on a good many of his trips with him. The country is so beautiful. They are about the happiest people you ever saw; he is quiet about it, but she is just bubbling over. He told me he *loved her* so much and is so proud of her. We are all delighted with him; he seems to fit in very nicely with our little family and even conservative "little Lydia" says he is all right and wishes you could all know him, and you know that's a good deal for her.

We did have such a happy Christmas, Jimmie had never hung up his stockings so I got a big thick woolen one of Jim's and hung it up on the parlor mantle; then Grace gathered up all sorts of little tricks to put in it. In the toe she put her present to him — a pair of gold sleeve buttons, one shiny new penny all done up in tissue paper, and put in a box a woolly monkey and a little white sheep for he has said so much about the Rocky Mountain Sheep; also candy, nuts, etc. Of course we had lots of fun over that. Jimmie was as enthusiastic as any one over Christmas; he and Grace went out shopping together and gave us each something.

● ● ● ●

In the winter of 1908, February 27th, James Henry Moser's older daughter, Grace, was married to James Milton Fetherolf, a young man in the U.S. Forest Service stationed in Ogden, Utah, but who had been called to Washington for three months each winter. The young couple remained in Washington until the middle of April when they left for Ogden where Mr. Fetherolf became head of the Department of Planting in District 4.

From J. H. Moser to Grace and Jim
Friday night — June 12, 1908

Dear Children:

Well, you "tetched" my heart today when your letter came saying "we do enjoy Dad's letters to the full."

Our beloved "snoozers" are snoozing — Lyd and Mamsy are in the hands of "Morpheus." We all went to bed about 10:30 — home from Mission Club picnic, full moon, perfect night; same old place, mouth of Piney Branch. I drank most a gallon of coffee that would float a chunk of lead, so I suppose I'll keep awake for a week. Had to get up to do something — this is it — 12:30 P.M.

I imagine "Jeb" saying to you, Jimmie, "Isn't it a pity Dad drinks, but then he is so entertaining, and *so* bright, so young, so kiddish; you'd never think he was an old man when he gets on one of his coffee 'Bats'."

Now I think this is enough for you for one evening. I'm writing an article (by request) on "Washington as an Art Center' for the *Washington Herald* and it's most done. Guess I'll just run it over and see if that don't make me sleepy.

Yours, happy (far as IKN reach) —
Dad

· WHITE · HOUSE ·

· WASHINGTON ·

Perishable Flowers.

keep from Frost and extreme Heat.

To *Miss Grace Moser,*

1773 G. Street. N.W.

Washington, D.C.

Feb. 27th 1908 —

Box top in which were sent a variety of flowers from the White House with President Theodore and Mrs. Roosevelt's cards for our wedding. I wore some of the white hyacinths in my veil. The wedding took place in the old First Congregational Church with Dr. Newman officiating and music by Dr. Bischoff at the organ. The church was decorated with palms and other plants from the Blount's greenhouse. There was a reception at the church and supper for the wedding party later at the apartment.

119

J. H. Moser

WEDDING PORTRAIT — 1908
GRACE MOSER FETHEROLF

SUNSET, MT. McINTYRE
To Martha. October 4, 1908.

I am just back after two weeks at Cornwall Plains. Stayed in a cunning little room with a fireplace at Miss Lindley's. I never did such a pile of good things nor ever had a better working spell of the same number of days. We have had a great September for work, three whole weeks without a drop of rain, balmy and mild. I was out at daybreak almost every morning and had accomplished things before breakfast. Am back here finishing up, and shall have the best bunch of stuff yet, to take back with me. You know the Corcoran has its great show this winter, and I expect to be ready with a large picture, best yet for me.

Washington Times. December 12, 1908.

Unexpected good fortune has come to James Henry Moser through the recent purchase by William T. Evans of his picture ''Mt. McIntyre'' for the Evans collection of the National Gallery. The recognition is well deserved. Mr. Moser is the first Washington artist to be honored by Mr. Evans with a selection of his picture for the collection of one hundred paintings by prominent American painters, to be known as the ''Evans Collection.''

''Mt. McIntyre'' in one particular, that of size, may be considered an ambitious painting for it is a large canvas. The subject, that of a valley in the deep shadows of night, with the realism heightened by the twinkling lights of homes, a majestic mountain outlined against the evening sky — a somewhat definite and placid cloud form brightened by the light of the moon which has not yet illumined the valley — is a composition directly in line with Mr. Moser's most distinguished work, although as a painter of mountain scenery at night Mr. Moser has not travelled so far as in his daylight effects of mountain tops wreathed in storm clouds, or dissolving mists.

MILLS & GIBB,
BROADWAY & GRAND ST.

NOTTINGHAM. 49 STONEY ST
PARIS. 43 RUE DE PARADIS.
ST.PIERRE-LES-CALAIS. 4 RUE NATIONALE.
ST.GALL. 1 TEUFENECTR.
PLAUEN. 10 BAHNHOF STRASSE.
BOSTON. 3 HAMILTON PLACE.
PHILADELPHIA. 1033 CHESTNUT ST.
BALTIMORE. 206 NORTH LIBERTY ST
CHICAGO. 167 ADAMS ST.
ST.LOUIS. BROADWAY & LOCUST ST.
SAN FRANCISCO. 1456 FRANKLIN ST.

New York 11 Dec 1908.

Dear Mr Moser:

I enclose cheque for $350. in payment for the water color "Carnival on Mirror Lake" which I bought for Mrs Evans and the oil "Sunset, Mt. McIntyre" — both without frames. Kindly acknowledge. The "Sunset" is to be included in the Evans National Gallery collection with the understanding that if later I see another 30 x 40 by you which I may like better, an exchange is to be made, even if I have to pay something additional.

I will have Peers Bros make a frame for the National Gallery picture and unless you prefer to have it sent to your studio, I will have the frame forwarded direct to the Corcoran Gallery.

With cordial regards to you and yours in which I am joined by Mrs Evans, I remain

Yours very truly,
William T. Evans

121

SUNSET — MT. McINTYRE — 1907 *(Oil on canvas, 30 x 40)*

J. H. Moser

From the ''Evans Collection'' of one hundred paintings by prominent American artists. Gift of William T. Evans to the National Museum of American Art, Smithsonian Institution, Washington, D.C. Currently on loan to U.S. Senate Dining Room.

STUDIO JANITOR AS ART CRITIC

Inspired by Cash Gift, Pronounces "Paintin' Pictures de Bes' Business fo' Geniuses."

Mr. James Henry Moser, of Washington, D.C., tells a capital story of his negro janitor's appreciation of a cash New Year's gift.

"When I handed him the money," said the artist in telling the story, "he became extravagant in his praise of my 'Mount McIntyre', which has been bought by Mr. Evans to add to the Evans Collction in the National Gallery.

" 'Yasser', he concluded in an outburst of enthusiasm, 'paintin' pictures am de bes' business dey is fo' geniuses!' "

**New York Herald
January 10, 1909**

Letter from James Henry Moser. May 2, 1909.

My dear Jimson:

Regarding Grace's trip east a year after her marriage. We are glad to have her come when home and friends are as she left them, and dear little Grandma will get a new lease on life from Grace's visit. We are fast, Mother and I, becoming "the old folks," and the days of rush and hustle for me are certainly past. I am not uncheerful about it. What would be the use? I've had my day and it's been glorious. I'm ready to take now what comes and be as useful and cheerful as I can be.

Ever affectionately, Dad.

Grace spent six weeks visiting the eastern relatives.

Letter from James Henry Moser. April 22, 1910.

Dear Chil'n:

No, no, dassent think out loud as I generally do when I write to you for I'm not in my usual optimistic mood! The weather is so lovely and the day so fine, but the ducats come so slow and the season runs only a month more — gives me much to be concerned about. Want to resolve never to be discouraged again. So many of us famous ol' men is a-dyin' off — there goes ol' Mark Twain, the brightest of them all! It didn't seem as if he could ever die — and then in Connecticut too! Seems like the old state is getting to be a bad one for a "pusson feelin' poo'ly." Somebody's got to be "it" in this perpetual game of tag. But there is no denying that the month of March is past, and you know what the old darkey said about living through that month — he generally lived through the rest of the year.

Hoping that all goes well with you, I am your ever D.B.

P.S. We are ideally fixed — couldn't be better. We are sure of that after a full winter in the new apartment, but I'm to have receptions next week, a small studio exhibition, and I dread the hustle. I simply cannot maintain the sustained energy I did formerly through one of these spells. Got to scare up buyers to tide me over the summer. To send Mom out to Utah after baby comes, May.

James Moser Fetherolf was born May 13th.

123

STORM CLOUDS

J. H. Moser

"COLONEL HENRY F. BLOUNT"

J. H. Moser

PORTRAIT OF COLONEL HENRY F. BLOUNT
Excerpts from letters to Martha
in Ogden, Utah. 1910.

July 20th. Got order for portrait of Col. Blount. Oil three-quarter length, $500.

Aug. 5th. Mom Blount, her sister-in-law, Mrs. Eames, and Rose were in this morning to see the drawing. Mom declared on sight, ''Isn't that fine!'' so she is fixed. I was fearful she might like some other pose better. Now they will not see it till it is done, in September, and I shall have to make only slight changes if any. Took them to the Gallery. They thought it was great to get in there when it was closed; Miss Willard was very nice to us. They enjoyed my talk on the pictures. I have promised to go out there Sunday to dinner.

Aug. 8th. Col. Blount here to lunch with me on the porch. Col. as happy as a kid! Canteloupe, a corker big and jus' right peaches and cream, ''Lott'' toast, Swiss cheese, and ginger ale. Everything A.1., and the toast made him sit up and take notice.

Letter to Martha.

Sept. Mom Blount was in and said ''Oh, Jim, it's fine! It's your chef d' oeuvre, I never saw a finer portrait.'' I said mildly, ''I told you I was sure the head was the best I had ever done.''

FOOTNOTE: The portrait of Henry F. Blount hangs over the fireplace in the Boardroom of the Willard Library in Evansville, Indiana. ''One of our most prized possessions.''

124

125

BLOUNT'S GREENHOUSE — 1892

J. H. Moser

May 20, 1910.

My Dear Jimson:

"Lydie" and I saw "Budgie" safely off on the train last night.

"And now we part as part we must
We take it not unkind
That she who goes is happier
Than we-alls she leaves behind."

How we did wish we were all going! Returning about ten from a trip to Georgetown, I discovered I had left my key inside. I almost envied the boy who, when his employer complimented him on always having his knife with him and asked how it was when so many of the older clerks didn't, replied, "Guess it's 'cause I only got one pair of pants."

How I should like to see that little bunch of monkey-faced wrinkles. The new "heir with the hair." Expect he'll be some "bigger than a minute" when I see him.

To Martha.

Dear Madam:

Don't praise that baby so dern much, you give me the "itch" (to see him), and you with the "shingles" and me with "the itch" is a fine state of things. Send me some photos. Dear me, Grace singing those precious old songs, more "itch" don't!

One of the "scattered family"
James Henry Moser.

July 28th.

Yes, we are scattered, but next winter oh my, won't it be fine to have Lydie here with us — then if we only had that kid and his folks in the next block! But that would be heaven and we don't get there till we're dead you know.

J. H. Moser.

THE MOSER BUNGALOW

Some time prior to 1909, Martha acquired some five acres of land belonging to the ancestral farm, from her brother, Samuel Scoville. It was a rocky pasture a short distance north of the farm house and the house the Mosers had once occupied. On Martha's pasture, on a hill above the other houses, was a large flat rock on which solid foundation, in the summer of 1909, was erected a large stone fireplace and chimney. This chimney stood through the summer of 1910 when Martha was visiting her daughter Grace in Ogden, Utah, and until the following spring 1911, when a comfortable bungalow was built around it.

In June of this year however, Moser was on the fine arts jury for an exposition in Atlanta, Georgia, and on his way home on the train he suffered what proved to be a slight stroke. He had no recollection of how he got home from the station upon his arrival in Washington, and seemed exhausted when he reached there. He spent several weeks resting, and at the end of that time was able to be out and get around. By the middle of July he was well enough to go to Cornwall with Martha where the studio-bungalow was ready to be occupied. This bungalow, though primitive, was the culmination of a life-long dream and it would be hard to find any two happier people than James and Martha in their own little home in the country they both loved.

They spent the rest of the summer there quietly and he continued to recuperate until late fall when they returned to Washington and he again took up his class at the Corcoran Gallery.

126

127

H Moser · 1912

THE MOSER BUNGALOW

J. H. Moser

GREATEST EXHIBITION
OF AMERICAN PAINTINGS
Washington Herald. Sunday, December 25, 1910.
James Henry Moser.

Merry Christmas, children! Some of you look pretty large, but never mind. I intend, all the same, to confine this talk to the younger ones on our first visit to the art gallery. We shall see the greatest exhibition of up-to-date American paintings in this country this winter. It is the Corcoran Gallery's ''Third biennial exhibition of oil paintings by contemporary American artists.''

Here we are in the stately vestibule. As we stand and view the interior, with its superb marble stairway in the very center of the gallery, we are impressed by its massive proportions, architectural beauty, and the dignified simplicity of these venerable white sculptured masterpieces of Greek art about us. Before we go upstairs where the pictures are, I wish to explain to you what ''impressionism'' the new kind of painting is, for you must understand something of it if you are to comprehend the difference between the ''old school'' and the ''new school'' of painting. The pictures upstairs are almost all ''new school,'' and the new school artists are ''impressionistic'' painters — ''plain air'' men they are sometimes called — but that term is not so comprehensive.

If, for instance, on a canvas is painted three round spots, two red and one yellow, against a background the upper half of which is dark green and the lower half white, that might be an impressionistic picture of three apples, two red and one yellow, lying on a white table-cloth, and the wallpaper behind them a dark green. These two red and one yellow spots stand for the apples, and the green tint for the background, and the white for the table cover. This impressionistic picture only tells a few facts.

The apples are circular and the wall green. The back of the table is a straight horizontal line. Two apples are red and one yellow and the table cover white. Now some artists think that quite enough to tell about the natural objects they are representing while other artists, particularly the older school, would paint those apples, that table, and the background so lifelike, you might think they were real and try to pick up the apples.

Painting things so real that they seem to exist right before you is very old-fashioned art, and considered unworthy nowadays, but when your parents were little children, pictures painted so real were the only kind anybody tried to paint.

Hats and clothes go out of fashion and look funny to us. Hats and clothes change fashions without reason, but for this change in the ''art fashion'' there is the very best of reasons. Good artists paint only the beauty they see in the things they look at, the beautiful forms, colors, hues, tints and tones they see in nature, and do not try to make things so real that they are more full of reality than beauty. We must be the judges of whether the artists here have been successful or not. So, you see, impressionism and realism make mighty differences in pictures.

Furthermore, if artists painted nature only ''dreadfully real'' they would be nothing more than a lot of machines, and pictures would be as much alike as snapshots with a kodak in the hands of a novice. It is this ability to discover the beautiful in nature and suppress all that is not beautiful which lifts a painter from the class we call mechanics and places him with the great original poets and musicians. We call them ''interpreters of nature,'' and when they show real genius for discovering beauty, we say they are ''inspired.''

128

LAKE MOHONK AND HOTEL — 1898

J. H. Moser

No one ever said that of Preyer, the famous German fruit painter, who painted a fly on a grape leaf so natural you would not believe it painted until you tried to brush it away and failed. Nor of the man who painted pictures of dollar bills so real that you were sure that if the glass were removed, you would find the bill actually there. Such painters were skilled mechanics.

Among some of the old Dutch painters who painted with this minute mimetic skill, there were some few exceptions, who added to this perfect work, interpretation and qualities of color which have imparted to their pictures a compelling and enduring charm.

Do you see the difference between realism and impressionism? Well, there is just one thing more to be made clear before we ascend the beautiful stairway to where the eight galleries are filled with pictures — 352 of them — and that is the ''plain air school'' which, after all the involved talk one hears, is nothing more than painting in a true natural key — normal nature justifies these painters. Think of the brown, yellow tone, varnished oil paintings all had until very recently. No one expected them to look otherwise until the great Frenchman, Monet, came along and painted straw stacks in the sunshine with blue shadows and skies as white as chalk.

Of course, there was a great protest, but he was right. Nature did look that way, and all of a sudden there was a great rush among the students and painters to go back to nature and begin all over again.

The notions about the old dingy, amber-toned pictures — so many of the world's masterpieces among them — being good art was discarded, and what freaks some of these new painters did! It makes one shudder to think of them, but the movement was in the right direction and the pictures upstairs seem like hundreds of open windows looking out upon some of the loveliest scenes one ever beheld. And, as the painters have only given us the beauty they saw, and enough realism to make us forget that it is a painted canvas we are looking at, we are thrilled with delight and feel the joy known only in the open air in beautiful places.

It is the same with pictures of scenes indoors. The fresh, clear colors are true to the real atmosphere, and the smokey, brown picture that looks as though it were under a thick coat of molasses is not to be found here. These may become so in time, but the artists mean that their paintings shall at least start out frank and sincere statements of nature as she appears to them.

To get their effects, many of these painters found that, by putting bits of color side by side on the canvas, they could get more brilliant, vibrating, and beautiful tints than by mixing them together and making the color they wanted before putting it on canvas. Some succeeded and many failed; but it is generally admitted that the most successful pictures are painted in that way.

Forty years ago people all enjoyed pictures and strove to learn about art, because they enjoyed good pictures from the very beginning. Now pictures are hard for the layman to understand, because artists paint only to please themselves and for a critical few who have made a study of painting.

131

OLD VIRGINIA FIREPLACE NEAR KEYSVILLE — 1887 *(Oil, 10 x 14)*

J. H. Moser

Description of the pictures.

Let us now turn to the left. Yes; that Japanese umbrella with those two young ladies in white sitting in its shadow, is fiery and discordant, but that is only a "stunt." Mr. Freisike is "showing off," just trying to make us see how deceptive he can make his canvas. It is a refined kind of scene painting. No; before you go closer, first stand here and look through the doorway at the picture. Fold your right hand as though you were grasping a broom handle, and, in this "crimped up" shape, place your hand to your right eye as if your hand were a short, hollow tube. Closing your left eye, look through the hole in your little fist with the other, while you count to ten. A fine thing to do with any painting you wish to see right.

What happens? Why, you are startled to find that it seems to be a real outdoor scene in dazzling sunlight, and not a painted picture at all.

Mr. Freisike had, two years ago, a small canvas here not more than two feet square, which was one of the choicest and most admired pictures in the whole show. He is, indeed, one of our most skillful painters, but this year his painting screams his skill and betrays his lack of taste.

This "Garden Parasol" of Mr. Freisike is so very noisy one can hardly hear the melody and sweetness of many another song, sung just as well, in this same room by singers just as skillful as he.

For proof of this, we have only to look beyond Mr. Freisike's to John W. Alexander's painting called "Sunlight," loaned to this exhibition by the Art Institute of Chicago. Here is a picture quite as big as "The Garden Parasol." A bit of sunshine falls upon the floor at the feet of a woman simply clad and very beautiful.

Form, face, and costume are altogether lovely, and the color is so refined and harmonious! Note the simplicity of the composition, there are no distracting details. This is the most nearly faultless and altogether adorable picture in the whole collection.

See how little it takes to make a great picture. One does not miss the things left out, and I am very sure I never should have found the woman herself, as she posed for the painter, so lovely as she appears in this masterful interpretation by America's greatest painter of women.

BOWL OF DAISIES

J. H. Moser

132

133

AUTUMN GOLD

J. H. Moser

A SECOND GRANDSON
AND LYDIA'S MARRIAGE

In the spring of 1912 the Moser household was made happy by a visit from their daughter Grace, with her little two-year-old, his granddaddy's namesake. He was a beautiful husky little fellow and an endless source of pleasure to all the family, especially his granddad, who brightened at once and seemed more like himself than in some time. Grace and the little James went to Cornwall with the family and stayed until September.

In November two important family events took place. On the twenty-second a second grandson, Samuel Scoville, was born in Ogden, Utah; and on the twenty-sixth Moser's younger daughter Lydia, was married to Elmer Vernon Griggs of Iowa, at the home in Washington. The wedding took place in the spacious living-room adjoining the equally spacious studio of the "G" Street apartment, and James was able to give his daughter away and enjoy the happy occasion.

Lydia and her husband lived on at the apartment, and the family passed a quiet winter. James continued his Corcoran class three afternoons a week, but aside from that, did very little professional work.

He and Martha went to their bungalow in Cornwall in June where early in July he received the following letter.

PANAMA-PACIFIC INTERNATIONAL EXPOSITION
SAN FRANCISCO
Office of the President.

July 9, 1913.

J. H. Moser, Esq.,
   1814 "G" Street,
     Washington, D.C.

Dear Sir:

Your distinguished service and devotion to the cause of the Fine Arts have given your name a noteworthy place not only in your profession, but in public regard. It is therefore with the liveliest appreciation of your past services that I request the privilege of appointing you a member of the committee for Pennsylvania and the South Atlantic States advisory to the Department of Fine Arts of the Panama-Pacific International Exposition.

It is proposed to give the Department opportunity for exhibiting the best of the treasures of the United States in painting and sculpture, consisting of a carefully selected group of Retrospective American works and paintings by foreign artists owned in the United States, as well as a thoroughly representative collection of the contemporary art of our country.

From your service on this Advisory Committee it will gain greatly in prestige and efficiency and I can assure you that your service upon it will be thoroughly appreciated by the management of the Exposition, and of real assistance to the Chief of the Fine Arts Department.

May we count on your acceptance of this appointment?

Very truly yours,
Chas. C. Moore
President.

135

"A BREAK IN THE STORM — BLUE RIDGE MOUNTAINS" — 1899

MEDAL FOR WATERCOLOR — CHARLSTON EXPOSITION 1902

J. H. Moser

MOSER'S DEATH — 1913

Feeling refreshed and like himself again in the brisk mountain air of Cornwall, James wrote a letter of acceptance to Mr. Moore; then he and Martha stayed on through the summer spending quiet, happy, days on their sunny hilltop, enjoying the changing light on lake and hills, or doing small tasks about the place. Lydia and Elmer were with them through August, but they stayed on through October only returning for the opening of the Corcoran School on November first.

They had been home but a short time when James suffered another stroke — a much more serious one, which left him paralyzed and without speech until he passed away in his studio a short time later, November 10th, with his beloved "Martha" and his daughter Lydia at his side.

He was taken to Cornwall and laid to rest in the little North Cornwall Cemetery where lie generations of his wife's forebearers whom he so much admired; and among the "Cornwall Hills" he loved so dearly and painted so well.

J. H. Moser

WINTER SUNSET

PANAMA-PACIFIC INTERNATIONAL EXPOSITION

107 Lindy House
University Dormitories
37th and Spruce Sts.
Philadelphia.

My Dear Mrs. Moser,

I am acting in behalf of the management of the Department of Fine Arts of the Panama-Pacific International Exposition — and I write to say that the directors feel that no exhibition of watercolors — which aims to represent the best watercolor work produced in our country in the last few years — is complete unless it includes a group of Mr. Moser's pictures.

Would it be possible to gather together such a group of six (6) of Mr. Moser's very best and most representative watercolors to send to San Francisco?

If you can get together such a group and are willing to allow them to go to California, I assure you it would please the management very much as well as give pleasure to great numbers of people.

I shall be glad to send you labels and instructions for forwarding pictures to California on hearing from you.

I am

Very sincerely yours,
George Walter Dawson.

November 27th, 1914

NOTE: The six pictures which Mrs. Moser sent to the Panama-Pacific Exposition in San Francisco were given an entire wall in one of the smaller galleries and were hung in a group, beautifully lighted; a gracious tribute to one of America's best loved artists.

137

A BIT OF CORNWALL LAKE — 1897

J. H. Moser

The Evening Star. February 6, 1914.
The Washington Water Color Club
Opens Its Exhibit.

. . . The place of honor is very appropriately given to a group of watercolors by the late James Henry Moser, who, for ten years, was president of the club. This group comprises six paintings all of which are very characteristic. One is of a mountain-top among the clouds, another is of fog lifting, another shows "Birdcliff Camp" in the Catskills; besides which there are a November sunset, a picture of Connecticut in October, and finally a transcription of winter woods. Each picture represents an entirely different mood in nature, but all collectively, form a most harmonious group. Mr. Moser felt and interpreted, with peculiar sensitiveness, the beauty to be discovered in transitory effects. His cloud and mountain pictures are most notable, as are his transcriptions of showers and his interpretations of sunset and twilight effects.

His pictures have tonal quality. In them values are beautifully related. Each is, in its way, a revelation, a personal discovery made manifest to all. And his whole message is not delivered on the instant, for whereas an immediate impression is created, the deeper significance is conserved. Thus his pictures indefinitely retain their charm. There is something moreover, very intimate about Mr. Moser's paintings. One cannot fancy that they were ever indifferently painted or that they were done other than from the love of the doing. They are not fragmentary nor experimental, but complete — brought to a deliberate conclusion — lovely glimpses of nature and sincere works of art.

EULOGY BY WALDO HIBBS
Washington Star. November 1913.

In the passing of James Henry Moser, painter, jurer, critic, Washington loses one who, in his daily going and coming in this community, exemplified industry, optimism, clean living, and the full use of one's talents. A modern, he believed in and did much for the cause of American art.

Whether or not realizing that, from two years back, he was a stricken man, it was in accord with his previous attitude toward life, that he bore broken health with fortitude and cheerful outlook, as he had borne reverses and surmounted obstacles in the earlier days of his career. Like his friend, Francis D. Millet, he was a worker, and he continued to plan and attempt. The machinery moved, but not with its accustomed ease and vigor.

Mr. Moser's ideals were no vague dream. He studied thoroughly and practiced unremittingly, kept close in touch with nature, saw to it that his sources of inspiration were pure and fresh, that he might the better take advantage of superlative moments. Hence, he often rose to fine heights of expression. This expression whether poetic, decorative, or pictorial, was varied; at times tender as in his interpretation of an evening solitude, crudely truthful as in his characterization of a bald pasture-land under a winter sky, dramatic, as in the rendering of a magnificent storm cloud and sweep of rain over a mountainside. He continually bore in mind the relation between art and nature as he understood them. His feeling for color was instinctive and his technique soundly based.

139

AFTERGLOW ON THE HILLS

J. H. Moser

As a man kindly, with a strong sense of humor, full of verve, with homely tastes, Mr. Moser was loved of many.

His life passed as there subsided in the evening sky that afterglow which he loved.
— WALDO HIBBS —

POSTSCRIPT

After James Henry Moser's death in 1913 Martha stayed on in Washington with daughter Lydia and Elmer Griggs, a patent attorney. The Griggs later moved to New York where Elmer had obtained employment with the Bell Telephone Laboratories and became their Attorney General before his retirement. They had four children — Martha, Robert, David and Margaret.

James Fetherolf left the Forest Service and he and Grace purchased the sixty acre farm in Pennsylvania from his Mother, where they moved in 1918 with their three boys — James, Samuel and Ralph, born the previous year. There was a little stone house on the farm that had once been the Store and Post Office for Fetherolfsville dating back to 1730; this they added to and modernized into a comfortable home. Here the boys grew up helping with the farm work and attending school.

Father ran the farm in the old German tradition and also added a nursery of blue spruces grown from seed brought from Utah. He loved to collect and restore antiques and attended all the farm sales. He built up a rare and beautiful collection which sold for good prices just before his death in 1952.

The Fetherolf's vacation was quite often spent in Cornwall with Aunt Lill and Uncle Sam Scoville at the old farm house or with Grandmother Moser at the little bungalow. Here they were joined by the Griggs family in picnics, swimming, boating and fishing at the lake.

There were many fascinating pictures and mementos of Grandfather Moser in the bungalow which was designed as a studio and had a big fireplace in the living room. Grandmother sold a few pictures over the years, but those that were left were divided between Grace and Lydia, before her death in 1941.

Grace was happy to be near her relatives and enjoyed her garden and flowers. She had studied voice and piano and continued to sing and play all of her life. After her husband's death she went to live with son James and there compiled the Moser story and made six scrapbooks from the small paintings and sketches.

Dr. Richard Wunder, Curator of Painting at the National Collection of Fine Arts of the Smithsonian Institution, read Grace Fetherolf's manuscript and became interested in having further research done on Moser.

Rosemary A. Breen was given a research assistantship and compiled a book, "The Landscapes of J. H. Moser," as her thesis for a Master of Arts degree at George Washington University.

Two other students at the university, Sheila Hanna Cantor and Tescia Ann Yonkers, arranged for an exhibition of Moser paintings as partial fulfillment of their Master's thesis requirements. They borrowed thirty-seven oil and watercolor paintings from the family, prepared a catalog and presented the exhibit at the University Library on January 3rd to 5th, 1968, which was very well attended and received.

Dr. Wunder was later transferred to the Cooper-Hewitt Museum of Design in New York City and Grace Fetherolf died October 16th of the same year. Her Moser biography and Rosemary Breen's thesis were never published, but have provided a major part of the text for the present volume.

As a child, Grandmother Moser gave me the cover picture, "Train At The Water Tank," which was painted near Chicago in 1893. The little round white dome in the background was one of the World's Fair buildings. This little picture has always been one of my special favorites.

I have always believed the Moser story should be told, so have edited it into stories to be illustrated with his beautiful pictures.

Samuel Scoville Fetherolf

141

POND WITH WATER LILLIES

J. H. Moser

HIGHLIGHTS OF MOSER'S CAREER

JAMES HENRY MOSER, artist, illustrator, teacher and writer, born 1854, died 1913. Highlights of Moser's professional career:

1875 — Opened his own studio in Toledo, Ohio.

1878 — Galveston, Texas. Made business trip north and sold 10 watercolors to Groupel & Co., New York, and 20 to Williams & Everett in Boston.

1879 — Vicksburg, Mississippi. Made negro sketches which he was able to sell to *Harpers, Century* and other magazines. Atlanta, Georgia — Joel Chandler Harris liked his work and commissioned him to make the negro sketches for the first Uncle Remus book published in 1881 which brought national recognition.

1887 — Washington, D.C. Made pen drawings for the New York daily newspapers.

1888 — Painted "The Deadly Still Hunt" and "Where the Millions Have Gone" for the Smithsonian exhibit at the Centennial Exposition of the Ohio Valley and Central States.

1890 — First Lady Caroline Scott Harrison purchased the picture "Sunny Morning at Salisbury Beach" which she hung in the White House and arranged for lessons in watercolor painting.

1895 — On trip to Europe he painted some of his finest watercolors of the little town of Bolkenhein (now in East Germany).

1898-1913 — Taught a distinguished class in watercolor in the Corcoran Art Gallery, Washington, D.C.

1907 — Moser was the first Washington artist to have a picture selected for the Evans Collection of 100 Best American Paintings by Prominent American Artists.

JAMES HENRY MOSER was a member of the American Water Color Society, the New York Water Color Club, and the Salmagundi Club in New York City. He was secretary of the Society of Washington Artists, 1898-1901, and was President 1897-1900, 1905-1913 of the Washington Water Color Club, Washington, D.C. Moser participated in exhibitions in the following cities:

New York, New York: The Salmagundi Sketch Club, First Annual Exhibition of Original Black and White Drawings, Sketches and Etchings, 1879. National Academy of Design, Annual Exhibition, 1881, 1882, 1884, 1885, 1889, 1890, 1895, 1901, 1902, 1907. American Water Color Society, Annual Exhibition, 1882-1885, 1887, 1888, 1890, 1891, 1893, 1894, 1899, 1901-1903, 1906-1910. The New York Water Color Club, Annual Exhibition, 1893, 1895-1898, 1900-1907, 1909, 1911, 1912. The Salmagundi Club, Annual Exhibition and Auction Sale, 1905-1908.

Washington, D.C.: Society of Washington Artists, Annual Exhibition, 1891-1913. Washington Water Color Club, Annual Exhibition, 1896-1915. (Received first Corcoran Prize in Fifth Annual Exhibition in 1900 and Parsons Prize in Eighth Annual Exhibition in 1903.) The Old Corcoran Art Gallery, Art Loan Exhibition in Aid of Charity, April 11-28, 1898. The Corcoran Gallery of Art, Exhibition of Oil Paintings by Contemporary American Artists, 1907, 1909, 1910. The National Gallery of Art, Paintings and Other Art Objects Exhibited on the Occasion of the Opening of the National Gallery of Art in the New Building of the United States National Museum, March 17, 1910.

Philadelphia, Pennsylvania: The Art Club of Philadelphia, Annual Exhibition of Water Colors and Pastels, 1891, 1895, 1905-1907. The Pennsylvania Academy of Fine Arts, The Philadelphia Water Color Exhibition, 1904-1912. Also the One Hundredth Anniversary Exhibition, 1905.

Boston, Massachusetts: Boston Art Club, Exhibition of Water Colors, Pastels and Works in Black and White, 1889, 1891, 1893, 1897, 1901, 1905, 1908. The Copley Society, Second Annual Exhibition, 1895.

Chicago, Illinois: World's Columbian Exposition, Department of Fine Arts, 1893. The Art Institute of Chicago, Annual Exhibition of Water Colors, Pastels and Miniatures by American Artists, 1900-1913.

Bridgeport, Connecticut: Bridgeport Public Library, Works of Artists in Water Color and Pastel, November 1894.

Baltimore, Maryland: The Municipal Art Society of Baltimore, Exhibition of Water Colors and Engravings, 1900.

Buffalo, New York: Pan-American Exposition, Exhibition of Fine Arts, 1901. Buffalo Fine Arts Academy, Albright Gallery, Annual Exhibition of Selected Water Colors by Contemporary American Artists, December 12, 1907-January 12, 1908; September 14-October 15, 1911. Also the Ninety-Fourth Annual Exhibition of Selected Paintings by American Artists, 1909.

Charleston, South Carolina: Charleston Exposition, 1902. (Received Bronze medal.)

Richmond, Virginia: Richmond Art Club, Spring Exhibition, 1901, 1902.

St. Louis, Missouri: Universal Exposition, 1904. The St. Louis Museum, The Annual Exhibition of Selected American Water Colors, 1906, 1907, 1909, 1910-1913. Also The Annual Exhibition of Selected American Paintings, 1907, 1908.

Portland, Oregon: Lewis and Clark Centennial Exposition, June 1-October 15, 1905.

Worcester, Massachusetts: The Worcester Art Museum, Exhibition of Water Colors and Pastels, March 29-April 19, 1908.

Knoxville, Tennessee: Appalachian Exposition, Section of Fine Arts, October, 1910 (Moser was the Advisory Director of the Section of Fine Arts and a member of the jury. He contributed to the exhibition by special invitation.)

San Francisco, California: Panama-Pacific International Exposition, Department of Fine Arts, 1915.